Fort Smith

On the Front Cover: The Free Bridge on the former Albert Pike Highway was dedicated on May 11, 1922. This 1924 postcard offers an eastern view of Garrison Avenue. This bridge allowed commerce and tourism to flow more freely between Arkansas and Oklahoma. Over 25,000 people attended the opening ceremonies, which were highlighted by a parade, speeches, numerous bands, fireworks, and an evening showcase of electric progress. (Fort Smith Museum of History.)

On the Back Cover: This 1911 postcard showcases the ornate buildings and meticulous gardens of Electric Park. Originally known as McCloud Park, the 75-acre area included a casino, an auditorium, two baseball fields, an elaborate greenhouse, and various carnival rides and attractions. The Fort Smith Light and Traction Company owned and operated the park until the 1920s. (Goff Collection, Pebley Center, University of Arkansas-Fort Smith Boreham Library.)

POSTCARD HISTORY SERIES

Fort Smith

Kevin L. Jones

ARCADIA
PUBLISHING

ISBN 978-0-7385-9065-3

Published by Arcadia Publishing
Charleston, South Carolina

Printed in the United States of America

Library of Congress Control Number: 2012942635

For all general information contact Arcadia Publishing at:
Telephone 843-853-2070
Fax 843-853-0044
E-mail sales@arcadiapublishing.com
For customer service and orders:
Toll-Free 1-888-313-2665

Visit us on the Internet at www.arcadiapublishing.com

Thanks go to my parents, my grandma, my brother, my wife, and our son. Special thanks go to my in-laws and friends, who introduced me to the history of Fort Smith. Thanks also go to all of my friends and family members for their encouragement.

Contents

Acknowledgments

This book would not have been possible without Caroline Speir and Leisa Gramlich of the Fort Smith Museum of History, the Pebley Center at the University of Arkansas-Fort Smith, Emily Lovick at the Fort Smith National Historic Site, the Fort Smith Public Library Genealogy Department, Lynn Wasson at *Entertainment Fort Smith* magazine, Stan Kujawa for his advice and access to his collection, Janie Glover at the Fort Smith Chamber of Commerce, and my family and friends, of course.

INTRODUCTION

History is alive in Fort Smith. Many unique individuals and events have been centered along Garrison Avenue and its nearby neighborhoods from 1817 to the present. From "Hell on the Border," as Judge Isaac C. Parker's jail was known, to the numerous businesses that have thrived along Garrison Avenue since the 1800s, this postcard history of Fort Smith connects the past with newly developed downtown businesses and planned growth.

The River Valley's collective memory looks forward to the past. With this motto as they live history and celebrate its deep connections, the citizens understand the implications of where previous generations have been. History means tourism dollars in one sense, but it also helps people identify themselves and each other, and it provides a sense of place as people move into the future.

Many problems encountered by the people of Fort Smith can be measured by how past citizens faced adversity, criticism, or change. Some locals are concerned about military bases closing, but a student of history knows that this issue has been on the minds of Fort Smith residents since the 1800s. Issues of immigration, the assimilation into an established culture, or the application of new skills and technology in an evolving workforce are also concerns previous generations had as they raised their children and thought about improving their quality of life and pursuing happiness.

History tells us that there is nothing new under the sun. It is egotistical to believe that our time is the best or the most important time in the history of Fort Smith. Yes, it is important to be positive about the present and hopeful for the future, but to think that our fears and dreams have not been similar to those who came before is naive; we should all make the world a better place because we are in it.

The postcards showcased in this book should encourage the belief that, in the words of the late C. Ray Baker, former Southside High School history teacher and mayor of Fort Smith, "Life is worth living in Fort Smith, Arkansas." Furthermore, these pages show the history of local churches, hospitals, and cultural centers.

These postcards follow the area's growth from its beginnings as a small fort near Belle Point to a federal courthouse and on to its development as one of the largest and most historically important cities in Arkansas. The city reflects its landscape, as it serves as a crossroads of river transportation, rail activity, and highways, all of which have been economic catalysts.

This book shows a people searching for stability, justice, opportunity, improvement, safety, contentment, and other American truths, from the earliest troops enforcing treaties between the Cherokee and the Osage to the numerous men and women who have toiled.

One

Belle Point, the First Fort, and the Origins of Fort Smith

This postcard was postmarked from Fort Smith on September 10, 1893. It passed through New York City on September 21 and arrived in Stuttgart, Wurttemberg, Germany, on October 3. It was sent to Joseph Pappenheimer in Stuttgart from a man known only as "Karl," who writes in German on the reverse side and was likely a relative of Jacob Pappenheimer, who owned a furniture store at 622 Garrison Avenue beginning in the 1870s. Sometime after 1893, Jacob moved to New York City, where he died at age 66 on December 9, 1902. (Stan Kujawa collection.)

The second Fort Smith, seen here before the Civil War, was the subject of this postcard, published in 1907 by the Fort Smith Art and Wallpaper Company and hand-colored in Germany. Visitors to the Fort Smith National Historic Site can investigate the original 1839 commissary building and the officers' barracks—which became Judge Isaac C. Parker's courthouse and federal jail—and walk to the site of the first Fort Smith foundation, begun in 1817 off Belle Point, within the Fort Smith National Historic Site. The sender of this card writes on the front, "This is before our time." (Fort Smith National Historic Site Postcard Collection.)

This 1909 postcard identifies the second Fort Smith quartermaster building incorrectly as the commissary building. The 1838–1839 structure no longer exists, although photographs and postcards reveal it still standing as late as the 1920s. This quartermaster building was at the south end, near the current gallows exhibit at the Fort Smith National Historic Site. (Fort Smith National Historic Site Postcard Collection.)

The building identified in this 1906 card as "Officer's Headquarters Old Fort Smith 1830" was actually the quartermaster building, which was constructed around 1838. Fort Smith's mission for many decades was to help keep the peace between Indian tribes by enforcing treaties while protecting local citizens from attacks. The first Fort Smith was constructed to maintain peace between the Osage and the Cherokee tribes. During the Civil War, Confederate troops held the fort from 1861 to 1863. Additionally, the strategic location was an important link in the military supply chain until 1871. (Fort Smith National Historic Site Postcard Collection.)

In the early 1900s, Bob McCann photographed downtown Fort Smith to make popular photograph-cards and hand-tinted postcards. In this 1923 view, a couple stands near the 1839 commissary building, which is now part of the Fort Smith National Historic Site. After the city purchased the building in 1898, the City Federation of Women's Clubs began the Fort Smith Museum of History in 1910. The Fort Smith Museum of History was housed here until 1979. The commissary remains one of the oldest structures in Fort Smith. Many of the buildings near the old commissary were destroyed by a tornado in 1996. (Fort Smith National Historic Site Postcard Collection.)

The Poteau River meets the Arkansas River at Belle Point, seen in this early-1900s postcard, which looks north toward the area where two keelboats landed 70 soldiers on December 25, 1817. The first Fort Smith, which served troops from 1817 to 1824, was named after the commanding officer, Thomas A. Smith. The fort foundation can still be viewed near this location as part of the Fort Smith National Historic Site. The second Fort Smith was constructed in 1838. (Fort Smith National Historic Site Postcard Collection.)

This 1908 postcard shows troops at Fort Smith during the Civil War. They are on the parade ground between the main barracks. The building on the left was destroyed by fire, the one in the background at center is the still standing commissary building, and the officers' barracks at right was converted to house a federal jail and courthouse in 1872. (Fort Smith Chamber of Commerce.)

This 1911 postcard shows Judge Isaac C. Parker's federal courthouse, jail, and gallows at Fort Smith. The wagon at the steps hauled lawbreakers from the Arkansas Western District and Indian Territory from 1872 until the early 1900s. The conditions of the basement jail were so miserable that it was known as "Hell on the Border." Judge Parker and Anna Dawes, the daughter of Sen. Henry Dawes, advocated for federal funds in 1885, resulting in a new jail in 1888. A three-story structure consisting of 24 five-foot-by-seven-foot cells, which held two prisoners each, was added to the existing courthouse. US marshals, jail officers, and court employees used the structures from 1872 to 1917. From 1920 to 1955, the Public Welfare Department and the Public Health Service operated here, as did a YMCA and a maternity ward for the poor. The Fort Smith National Historic Site was created in 1961 and dedicated in 1964. (Fort Smith National Historic Site Postcard Collection.)

Isaac Charles Parker, a native of Ohio who later moved to Missouri, served two terms in the US House of Representatives and became one of the most effective federal judges in history. Parker was thought of by many as only the "Hanging Judge," but he also helped "civilize" Fort Smith by serving on school boards, encouraging businesses, hospitals, and churches, and promoting a better quality of life for all. He served for 21 years on the federal bench, often keeping his court in session six days a week and 10 hours a day. He is buried in Fort Smith National Cemetery. (Fort Smith Public Library Genealogy Department Postcard Collection.)

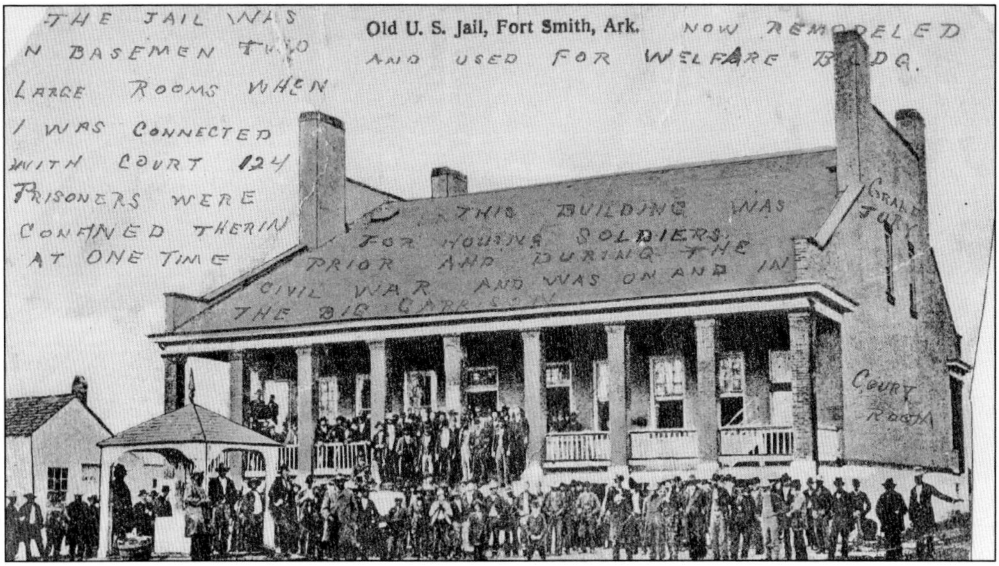

This 1911 postcard is believed to have belonged to Edward Haglin (1862–1951), who was commissioned as a deputy marshal on February 21, 1888, under US marshal Jacob Yoes. The scene shown on the card occurred between 1872 and 1888. The handwriting on the front and reverse is presumed to be Haglin's. The front reads: "The jail was [i]n basemen [*sic*]. Two large rooms when I was connected with court 124 prisoners therin [*sic*] at one time. This building was for housing soldiers during the Civil War and was on and in the big garrison. Deputy Marshals, attaches of court witness and hangers-on." Additionally, he writes about the "court room," the "grand jury," and how the building was "now remodeled and used for welfare building." Haglin wrote on this card between 1911 and his death in 1951. (Fort Smith National Historic Site Postcard Collection.)

The reverse of the 1911 Haglin card reads, "Property of Edward Haglin" and "The courtroom was on the right half of first floor. Left half was cut up in half for marshals and clerk. Prisoners were confined in two large rooms beneath. One time there were 137 confined there. The grand-jury met up where the two windows show." (Fort Smith National Historic Site Postcard Collection.)

The Sixth Street post office and courthouse in Fort Smith is seen on this postcard from the so-called White Border era, meaning it was printed between 1915 and 1930. Judge Isaac Parker's court moved to this building in 1890, and Parker served as a federal judge here until 1896. Prisoners were housed and court offices remained at the older court building until 1917. Parker died from Bright's disease and exhaustion on November 17, 1896. (Fort Smith Public Library Genealogy Department Postcard Collection.)

After a series of storms and a fire damaged the 1890 post office and courthouse in the 1930s, a modern building took its place. The new structure, on Sixth Street, is labeled the "Isaac C. Parker Federal Building" on this 1950s postcard. Some furniture and items from Parker's original courtrooms (1875–1896) can be seen at the Fort Smith National Historic Site. (Fort Smith Public Library Genealogy Department Postcard Collection.)

Fort Smith has benefited economically from Arkansas River traffic since the 1800s. This 1920s postcard shows the *Border City*, a freighter piloted by Capt. B.C. Blakely. In 1927, according to the reverse of this postcard, Captain Blakely's daughter, Mary, told that this boat was a gasoline-powered version of an earlier steam-driven boat her father had used on the Arkansas River. Captain Blakely was helping the US government build a jetty near Van Buren when this boat burned in 1907. (Fort Smith Public Library Genealogy Department Postcard Collection.)

Steamboats and freight boats of all sizes were common in Fort Smith in the 1800s and early 1900s. Significant barge traffic continues on the Arkansas River Navigation System today. This postcard from around 1900 shows a thriving boat dock. "Jack" was a local boat repairman who also "kept boats for hire." This was also near a "catamaran swimming pool" at the mouth of the Poteau River where many attended swimming classes. (Fort Smith Public Library Genealogy Department Postcard Collection.)

Between 1907 and 1930, many postcards were produced of this east view of Garrison Avenue. Some were black-and-white, hand-tinted prints or sepia-tone postcards, yet few historians agree on a date for this card. A few title it as 1870, while others suggest it was 1863. Immaculate Conception Catholic Church, the white structure at the end of street, was built in 1867, ravaged by the 1898 tornado, and later used as a parish hall before eventually forming St. John's Mission on Midland Boulevard. Businesses dot either side of the wide thoroughfare. Today, Immaculate Conception's brick structure, dedicated June 1, 1899, is still at the head of Garrison Avenue, which remains a vital artery of culture and commerce. (Fort Smith Chamber of Commerce.)

This 1914 view shows Garrison Avenue looking west toward Oklahoma near the current site of the J. Fred Patton Bridge, which was built in the 1970s. The Missouri Pacific Railroad Bridge is at the left. The Frisco depot and the old commissary building of the second Fort Smith are to the south out of the shot. Fort Smith had 2,227 people at the time of the 1870 census, 11,311 by 1890, and 23,975 by 1910. Much of the population growth was a direct result of new laws enacted by US marshals after 1889, when Oklahoma Territory was open for settlement and Fort Smith became a transportation hub for river and train traffic. (Fort Smith Chamber of Commerce.)

William Henry Harrison Clayton lived in the house (top of card) on Sixth Street in the historic Belle Grove District of Fort Smith during his time as a US district attorney in Judge Parker's court. Clayton was later appointed a federal judge in McAlester, Oklahoma. He is buried in the Fort Smith National Cemetery. This house is in the National Register of Historic Places and is open to the public. Visitors have encountered paranormal experiences—including voices, apparitions, smells of lilac perfume, and other unexplainable phenomena—while at the Clayton House. Miss Laura's Social Club (bottom of card) is a former bordello and restaurant that now serves as the official Fort Smith Visitor Center. This structure was one of seven houses of ill repute originally on "The Row" near the Arkansas River in 1900. An oil-tank explosion destroyed many of the seven houses in 1910. Northwest of Garrison Avenue, Miss Laura's is a stop for visitors interested in how "social clubs" operated in Fort Smith around 1900. (Fort Smith Public Library Genealogy Department Postcard Collection.)

This 1910 postcard looks west down Garrison Avenue in 1897. The popular Boston Store is on the left side of the street. The years between 1875 and 1929 were an era of great progress for the city. Trolley cars began lines in Fort Smith in 1883. The sender of this postcard, in a letter to her nephew in Michigan, notes, "It is so hot, I can scarcely see to write—and awful dry." (Fort Smith Public Library Genealogy Department Postcard Collection.)

A tornado devastated Fort Smith at 11:15 p.m. on January 11, 1898, leaving $450,000 in damages (in 1898 dollars). The tornado killed 55 people and injured 113 as it ripped through, destroying much of the Fort Smith National Cemetery, Belle Point School, Garrison Avenue, Eight and Twelfth Streets, Texas Corner, Towson Avenue, the Central Methodist Church, the First Baptist Church, and Brownscombe Methodist Church. It also damaged the three-month-old high school building, which had cost $50,000 to build. This postcard is one of a series of cards made and sold by M.H. Mark's Clothing Store of Fort Smith in 1898. (Fort Smith Chamber of Commerce.)

The newly constructed Fort Smith High School was nearly destroyed in the 1898 tornado and was refurbished three more times between then and 2011. Today, Darby Junior High School is at this location. Tornadoes in 1898, 1927, 1966, and 1996 battered Fort Smith and area towns such as Alma, Van Buren, and Greenwood. The resilience of the people in this area shows true grit. (Fort Smith Chamber of Commerce.)

Two

Progress, Peace, and Prosperity

A mixture of frontier town and modern city is seen here looking west sometime after 1909. The shot is dated by the tall, white First National Bank of Fort Smith on the left. The iconic brick building remains one of the largest and most recognizable features of Garrison Avenue. (Fort Smith Chamber of Commerce.)

This postcard from the early 1900s demonstrates how Fort Smith Light and Traction (FSL&T) Company linemen maintained the city's arc streetlamps. Although it began as a technological and economic leader in the area, the company had financial and legal troubles in the 1920s and became a subsidiary of Oklahoma Gas and Electric. (Fort Smith Chamber of Commerce.)

This group is off to the Fort Smith fairgrounds in 1904. Between 1902 and 1933, many rode the trolley for 5¢. The first electric streetcars appeared in 1893 and 33 miles of track were eventually laid. The Fort Smith L&T Co. Express line's car no. 24 is seen here. The FSL&T operated routes to Van Buren and Arkoma as well as lines from Grand Avenue to Waldron Road, Towson Avenue to Arkoma, and Twenty-first Street to the old fairgrounds at what is now Ramsey Junior High on Jenny Lind Road. In 1933, when city bus service took over, the Oklahoma Gas and Electric shut down the streetcars. Thanks to the efforts of Dr. Art Martin, Charles Winters, the Fort Smith Streetcar Restoration Association, and numerous volunteers and donors since 1979, Fort Smith now has a unique trolley museum that operates four of the original 58 streetcars on short routes near downtown. Additionally, trains and exhibits from Frisco, Burlington Northern, and other railroads are open at the Fort Smith Trolley Museum, on Fourth Street. The Arkansas & Missouri Railroad also offers scenic tours beginning near the trolley museum or from downtown Van Buren's historic depot to Winslow and Northwest Arkansas. (Fort Smith Chamber of Commerce.)

On this postcard, with a view looking east on Garrison Avenue, the owner, "Walter," writes, "A busy day in this town"—an apt description of Fort Smith between 1899 and 1929. This postcard shows the Hotel Main, built in 1885, to the right. The First National Bank would erect its new building next to the hotel in 1910. (Fort Smith Chamber of Commerce.)

The Missouri Pacific Railroad Bridge, also known as the Iron Mountain/Helen Gould Railroad Bridge, was dedicated in 1891. This postcard view was taken in 1915. The abundance of coal in the areas to the south and west encouraged railroads to flock to Fort Smith. The bridge offered both rail service and pedestrian crossing into Indian Territory, as Oklahoma would not become a state until 1907. This bridge was an integral part of importing and exporting people, goods, and services until the 1960s, when it was removed to improve the Arkansas River Navigation System. (Fort Smith Chamber of Commerce.)

This 1918 postcard advertises the First National Bank of Fort Smith, at Sixth Street and Garrison Avenue. The bank originated in 1872 with a partnership between Fort Smith Oil and Cotton Company members Bernard Baer and Logan H. Roots and businessmen Richard C. Kerens, Elis S. Mitchell, Dr. E.R. Duvall, and Arthur Gunther. Original directors of the bank included George T. Sparks, Samuel McLoud, and James Vaile, who created the first large furniture factory in the area—McLoud, Vaile, and Sparks. McLoud's son-in-law A.N. Sicard was the first of four generations of Sicards to lead the bank. These families continue to influence many industries in the River Valley, including medicine, education, real estate, and economic development. (Fort Smith Chamber of Commerce.)

This view on Sixth Street looks north from Rogers Avenue and offers clues about Garrison Avenue prior to the brick paving of city streets in 1914. Only a few buildings in this postcard still stand, including the First National Bank of Fort Smith on the right. (Fort Smith Chamber of Commerce.)

Fort Smith's Union Station Depot is seen here in 1915. Built two years earlier, it was located at the site of the present-day Fort Smith Convention Center on Rogers Avenue. The depot serviced the Kansas City Southern and Frisco railways for many years. After passenger service declined nationwide in the 1960s, many beautiful depots like this one were abandoned or demolished. (Fort Smith Public Library Genealogy Department Postcard Collection.)

"The Commercial Heart of Fort Smith" is seen in this aerial postcard from 1922. Many unique structures that still stand are shown, including the New Theatre at Tenth Street (right), built in 1911; the Friedman-Mincer Building (right) at Texas Corner (Towson and Garrison Avenues), built in 1915; and the Merchant's Bank, which housed H.B. Caldwell's insurance offices for much of the early 1900s. Lewis Friedman came to America from Hungary in 1888 and operated a beer distributorship and a tobacco store on Garrison Avenue and Sixth Street. Additionally, Friedman was postmaster from the 1930s until 1944. Silas Mincer was a local merchant who died in the 1898 tornado. Today, the Friedman-Mincer Building has been subjected to water damage from severe storms and its future is unclear. (Fort Smith Chamber of Commerce.)

Seen here in 1915, the train bridge linking Fort Smith to Van Buren was completed by the Kansas City Bridge Company in 1912. Construction of the 1,760-foot bridge lasted for 15 months and cost $650,000. Built with two sets of tracks, to accommodate steam locomotives and streetcars, this bridge allows river traffic passage under its seven sections at various points and continues to serve Fort Smith and Van Buren. The opening title sequence of the 1988 film *Biloxi Blues*, starring Matthew Broderick, begins with a historic Van Buren passenger car crossing the Arkansas River on this bridge. The car is part of the Arkansas & Missouri Railroad now. Portions of Van Buren, Fort Smith, and Fort Chaffee were also used in the making of the film. (Goff Collection, Pebley Center, University of Arkansas-Fort Smith Boreham Library.)

In the early 1900s, the extensive flower garden at Fort Smith's Electric Park was the envy of many such parks. This view shows what trolley patrons would see upon arrival at this stop. Park owners hoped to encourage families to spend time and money here. To the right were a casino, ballfields, and picnic areas. (Fort Smith Public Library Genealogy Department Collection.)

This view of Garrison Avenue looks west in the early 1910s and shows the hustle and bustle of the city's center. At the right, the Merchant's Bank, now the site of Fort Smith's city offices, flies a flag, and the Hotel Main and First National Bank of Fort Smith are on the left. (Fort Smith Public Library Genealogy Department Postcard Collection.)

Bob McCann's photograph company is at the right, opposite S.H. Kress & Co. 5-10 and 25¢ Store. McCann created many postcard views of Fort Smith in the early 1900s. Kress would remodel its store in the 1930s. Today, the building is under development for new opportunities. This view also shows the Joie Theatre, built around 1920, on the left, and Davis Drug Store on the right, west of McCann's. The Joie Theatre was one of the largest vaudeville and movie houses in the area until a 1953 fire. After interest grew in the new movie theaters at Central Mall and later at the Phoenix Avenue Mall, the Joie's location became a parking lot. (Fort Smith Public Library Genealogy Department Postcard Collection.)

This 1909 postcard shows the Kress Store and its 17 employees. The Boston Store, another iconic Fort Smith store, which operated from the 1800s until 1986, is to the left. Among the various items for sale at the Kress Store were many of the postcards featured in this book. Most postcards of Fort Smith between 1900 and 1950 were sold by the Kress Store and S and S News Service. (Fort Smith Museum of History.)

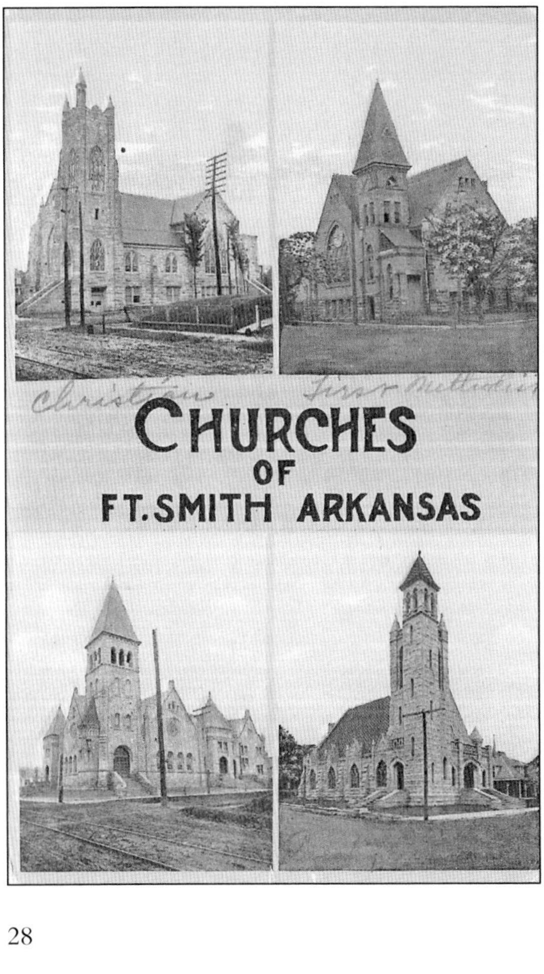

This postcard, "Churches of Fort Smith," was published by the Commercial Colortype Company of Chicago in 1918. Shown, clockwise from upper left, are the First Christian Church, the First Methodist Church, the First Baptist Church, and the Presbyterian Church of Fort Smith. (Fort Smith Public Library Genealogy Department Postcard Collection.)

The Church of the Immaculate Conception, seen in this 1908 postcard, reminds current residents of the long association of this towering structure at the eastern end of Garrison Avenue. The current church building was dedicated in 1899 and, with its large membership, continues many long-standing traditions, including its annual spring festival. The church's elementary school, which is nearby and offers preschool through sixth grade, was built in 1930 and has provided a strong foundation for many citizens of Fort Smith. St. Boniface and Christ the King Catholic Churches also have long ties to the area, with each having its own school as well. (Goff Collection, Pebley Center, University of Arkansas-Fort Smith Boreham Library.)

St. Anne's Convent of Mercy faces Rogers Avenue directly behind the Church of the Immaculate Conception. This 1905 building was the third convent structure for the Sisters of Mercy in Fort Smith. Irish clergy established St. Patrick's parish in the 1840s, with the first parochial school, St. Anne's Academy, opening in 1853. The 1905 convent was built near the site of Pres. Zachary Taylor's home. Taylor was commander of Fort Smith for a time prior to his service as a general in the Mexican War and his presidency. After an 1875 fire destroyed the home, which served as a school and convent for a time, a grotto was established in the remains of the chimney. The chimney still stands today, as does this 1905 structure, but renovations are needed to prevent the building from falling into ruin. (Fort Smith Public Library Genealogy Department Postcard Collection.)

St. Anne's Academy served Fort Smith from 1853 to 1973. The Sisters of Mercy built their first school in Fort Smith in 1869, offered a boarding school throughout the 1800s and early 1900s, and ran a high school from the 1920s until 1973. This postcard was printed between 1915 and 1933. (Fort Smith Public Library Genealogy Department Postcard Collection.)

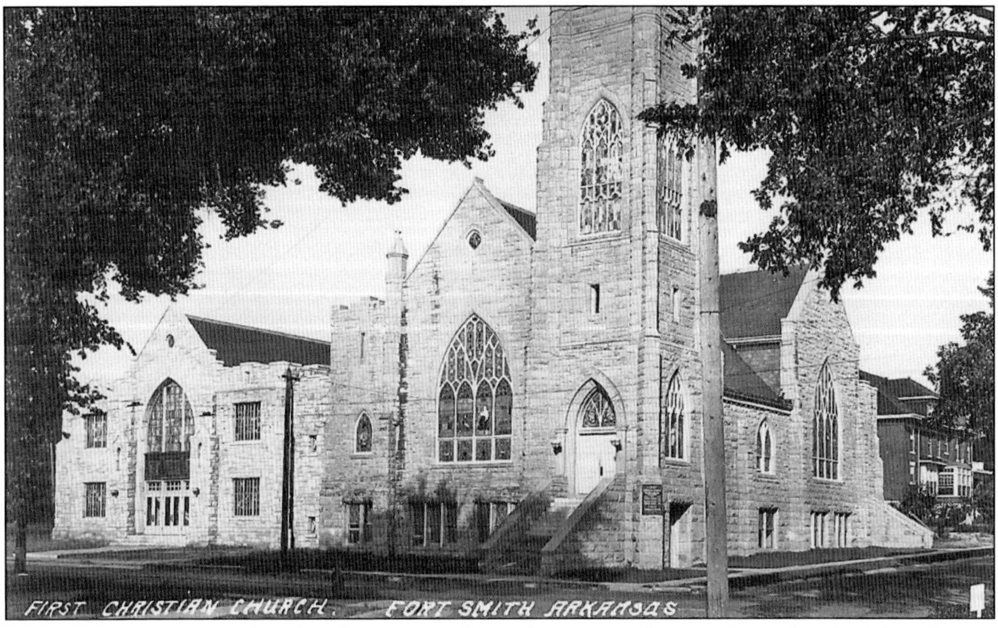

The First Christian Church of Fort Smith is shown in this 1918 card. The church was established in 1854 in Fort Smith. This structure, the congregation's third, was dedicated in 1905. The First Christian Church (Disciples of Christ) moved to its present location at Free Ferry and Rogers Avenue in the 1960s. (Fort Smith Public Library Genealogy Department Postcard Collection.)

The First Methodist Episcopalian Church, seen here in the 1920s, was first occupied in 1921 and was dedicated in 1938 at North Fifteenth Street. In the 1830s, circuit riders came to the church to preach; today, the First United Methodist Episcopalian Church continues at the renovated complex. (Fort Smith Public Library Genealogy Department Postcard Collection.)

The First Baptist Church of Fort Smith was founded in 1857. This 1908 postcard shows the church's third structure, built in 1899. The second building had been near the new 1898 high school, but it was destroyed during the massive tornado and only the "Cyclone Bible" survived. The congregation built its current home in 1968, not far from the second building site, across from what is now Darby Junior High School (the former Fort Smith High School). (Fort Smith Public Library Genealogy Department Postcard Collection.)

The Fort Smith National Cemetery, established in 1867, began as the first fort cemetery in 1818. The 1898 tornado damaged the superintendent's lodge and outer walls. The current administration building was constructed in 1904, and the Victorian gates were moved from the main entrance to the southern boundary in 1942. (Fort Smith Museum of History.)

This postcard from around 1915 shows a view of the Fort Smith National Cemetery looking south toward the administration building and main gate. The AMVETS (American Veterans) group dedicated a carillon in 1986, and a Vietnam Veterans Memorial was added in 1998. There are 473 Confederate soldiers buried here, including Brig. Gen. James McIntosh and Alexander Steen. Judge Isaac Parker, William H.H. Clayton, and Gen. William O. Darby are also interred at the Fort Smith National Cemetery along with veterans of the wars in Iraq and Afghanistan. (Fort Smith Museum of History.)

Fort Smith operated one of the largest cottonseed oil and baling operations in the South. Cotton allowed many locals to become wealthy, including those who established the First National Bank of Fort Smith in 1872. In this image from around 1920, bales near the Arkansas River await trains and boats to be transported to worldwide markets. In 2011, Arkansas ranked sixth nationally in cotton production. (Fort Smith Chamber of Commerce.)

The Sebastian County Courthouse was built in 1889 for $55,000. The building also served as a city hall and municipal court and a jail for a time. A Confederate monument added in 1903 was originally intended for the Fort Smith National Cemetery, but it was not allowed to be put there due to national policy at the time. An Art Deco structure replaced this courthouse in 1937. (Fort Smith Public Library Genealogy Department Postcard Collection.)

This 1937 building, now in the National Register of Historic Places, replaced the 1889 courts facility and contained the city hall, the county courthouse, county offices, a jail, and municipal courts. It was constructed of limestone by the Works Progress Administration (WPA) for $490,000. In recent decades, the Confederate monument was joined by a Confederate States of America flag and monuments to local veterans as well as markers for the Butterfield Overland Mail stage routes through Fort Smith. In 2009, a new Sebastian County Courts Building was opened on B Street at a cost of $13 million. The Justice Center now holds six circuit judges and staff, the prosecuting attorney's office, the circuit clerk, and three district court judges and their staffs. (Fort Smith Public Library Genealogy Department Postcard Collection.)

This Masonic temple was dedicated in 1929 on North Eleventh Street. It replaced the previous Baer Memorial Temple, which had been engulfed by fire in 1919. The previous temple, at North Sixth and C Streets, was built in 1870. The long time span between the fire and the dedication of the 1929 temple was a result of cooperation between the multiple lodges in Fort Smith to make one area meeting place for all. The building was placed in the National Register of Historic Places in 1992. Since 2003, the temple has been known as the Western Arkansas Scottish Rite Temple. (Fort Smith Museum of History.)

Fort Smith High School was constructed in 1897, decimated by the January 1898 tornado, and then rebuilt and renovated by 1900. A 1912 fire also damaged portions of the newest addition (to the right in this 1914 postcard). The section at right remains as a central part of the building, which now houses William O. Darby Junior High School. (Fort Smith Museum of History.)

The "new" Fort Smith High School was completed in 1928 at Twenty-third and B Streets. Fort Smith's population was over 30,000 at the time and 848 students enrolled in the school, which was built to hold 3,000 students. The 1,060-seat auditorium has been a draw for many, on top of the strong academics and extracurricular activities. Student enrollment in recent years has topped 1,200. This building was shared by Fort Smith Junior College until 1950, when the small college expanded to the west side of Fort Smith, first as Westark Junior College. After many changes through the years, it became the University of Arkansas-Fort Smith in 2001. UAFS enrollment has since exceeded 7,000 students. (Fort Smith Public Library Genealogy Department Postcard Collection.)

The Fort Smith Fortnightly Study Club founded the Fort Smith Library in October 1891. Mary Parker, the wife of Judge Isaac Parker, was the study club board's president in 1888. When the 1898 tornado demolished the Parkers' home on North Thirteenth Street, Mary moved to Durant, Oklahoma, to live with her son, Charles. Andrew Carnegie gave a $25,000 grant, which, combined with a city tax for libraries, helped Fort Smith establish the first Carnegie library in Arkansas in 1908. (Fort Smith Library Genealogy Department Postcard Collection.)

Fort Smith maintained the Carnegie library until a larger location was built on South Eighth Street in 1970. A larger main branch of the Fort Smith Public Library opened in 2001 on Rogers Avenue across from Creekmore Park. Additionally, three more neighborhood branches have been built in the last decade, expanding opportunities for all to enjoy the library. Fort Smith and Eureka Springs are the only Carnegie libraries in Arkansas and are two out of the 1,679 that the steel magnate helped create nationwide. More than half of the original libraries, which opened between 1889 and 1946, are still in use. Fort Smith's Carnegie library is now home to Channel 5 KFSM-TV. (Stan Kujawa collection.)

Belle Point Hospital, seen here in 1903, is now the site of Sparks Ambulatory Center on Towson Avenue. The $35,000 hospital was the result of a merger between St. John's and City Charity Hospitals in 1899. St. John's was Fort Smith's first hospital in 1887. Belle Point became Sparks Memorial Hospital in 1908 after George Sparks donated $25,000 in memory of his wife, Ann Dibrell Sparks. (Stan Kujawa collection.)

Colonial Hospital, seen here in this early-1930s postcard, opened in 1928 on the "cooperative plan," which provided medical visits, surgery, and room and board for $2 a month. (Stan Kujawa collection.)

This St. Edward's Mercy Hospital building was established in 1905 by the Sisters of Mercy near St. Anne's Academy and St. Anne's Convent in Fort Smith. The hospital and a school of nursing operated here until 1975, when the current Mercy Fort Smith was constructed at Seventy-fourth Street and Rogers Avenue, at a time when few businesses were located there, and now offers more than 400 beds and employs more than 2,100 people. (Stan Kujawa collection.)

Sparks Memorial Hospital opened in 1953 with 150 beds at 1311 South I (or Eye) Street. Sparks had 185 beds at the time of this late-1950s postcard and offered a school of nursing, medical technology, and X-ray technology, as well as being home to Sparks Manor, a senior citizens' center. In 1966, it expanded to 326 beds, and in 1971, it became the largest hospital in Arkansas. An innovator in medical sciences, encouraging new procedures and technologies, Sparks completed a $40 million renovation of its facility in 2008. (Stan Kujawa collection.)

Fort Smith Lumber Company cut Ouachita virgin pine from 1908 to 1928 in Yell County and operated logging camps throughout Sebastian County and parts of Oklahoma, as well as a rail operation near Plainview in Yell County. Rose Creek Railway Company hauled logs into Fort Smith for the lumber company from Abbott, in Scott County. Much of the area near Petit Jean Mountain that was owned by the company was sold to help create Petit Jean State Park. Fort Smith Lumber Company closed its Plainview operations in 1928 due to tax difficulties. (Stan Kujawa collection.)

The Boston Store was a longtime fixture in Fort Smith, beginning in 1879 as the Baer Brothers store, a specialty store organized by Julius and Sigmund Baer and Aaron Puller. In 1892, it was sold to Rudolph Ney, who established the Garrison Avenue location. Ney's attention to detail and customer service endeared the store to many. The store moved to Central Mall in 1971 and closed in 1986. This 1909 postcard showcases the ladies' suit department. The Fort Smith Museum of History has offered a Boston Store Tea Room recreation and fashion show frequently since 2009 to remember the influence the Boston Store had on so many residents. Currently, there are no Boston Stores south of Kentucky. (Fort Smith Museum of History.)

The Boston Store offered many unique items to customers, including products from the "Fancy Linen and Art Goods Department," seen here. The store also had a carpet department as well as clothing and goods that customers in Fort Smith could not find anywhere else in the early 1900s. In 1922, the store was described as "one of the leading mercantile enterprises of the state and the largest in Fort Smith." Special mention is made in the *Centennial History of Arkansas*, which cites the "beauty of the display, the honorable methods of the house and the earnest effort put forth to please the customers." (Stan Kujawa collection.)

This 1908 postcard of the W.L. Friend Store, at 322–324 Garrison Avenue, highlights the retail department. The store offered newspapers, postcards, and sundries. It later became Fort Smith Seed Company. (Stan Kujawa collection.)

Fort Smith Biscuit Company was opened in 1880 by Christian "Carl" Wortz Sr. at 201 South Fifth Street, largely because of the influence of the trains in the area. He changed the name to Wortz Biscuit Company, in 1929, and eventually to Wortz Co. (Fort Smith Public Library Genealogy Department Postcard Collection.)

This postcard was made in Aurora, Missouri, around 1940. By this time, Wortz Co. had expanded its main bakery and offices to three buildings in Fort Smith and patented "Ten-Der-Rist Extra-Thin Crackers in the Foil Wrapper." Wortz developed branch bakeries and distributors in Little Rock, Texarkana, Tulsa, Oklahoma City, Fort Worth, Memphis, Tyler (Texas), Monroe (Louisiana), and Birmingham (Alabama). The Wortz family moved the company to Poteau, Oklahoma, in the 1980s, and it was sold to Ralcorp of St. Louis in 1997. In 2012, the Bremner Cracker (a subsidiary of Ralcorp) manufacturing plant closed. (Stan Kujawa collection.)

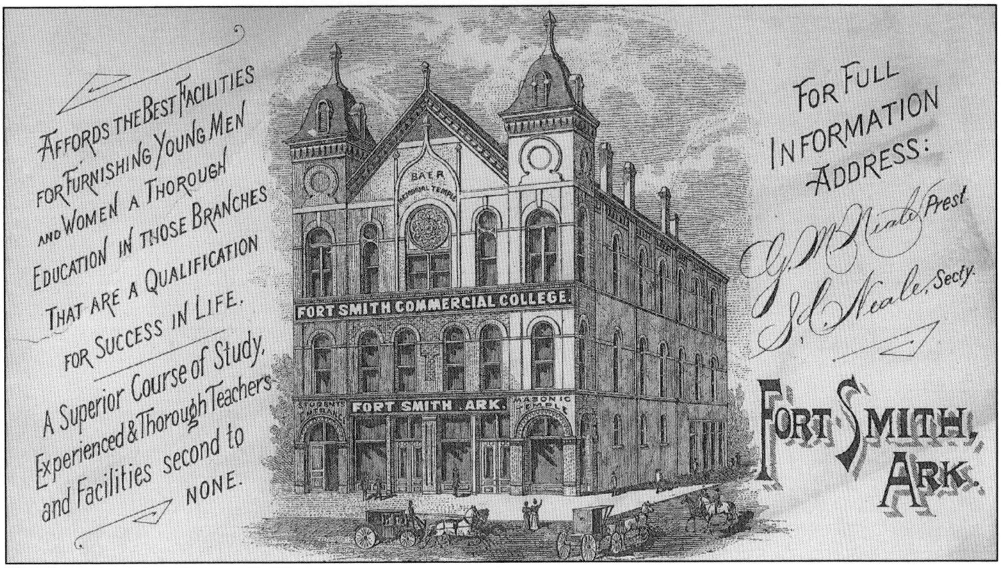

The Baer Memorial Masonic Temple at Sixth Street and Rogers Avenue was dedicated on December 6, 1889. It was ruined by fire in 1919. This 1917 postcard advertises Fort Smith Commercial College, which held classes "considered to be the best equipped in Arkansas and . . . perhaps the most widely known business college in this part of the country." B.A. Griswold, an accounting professor from Missouri, operated the school with the Neale family. At the time, students from 11 different states were enrolled. (Fort Smith Public Library Genealogy Department Postcard Collection.)

The Neale Commercial College evolved out of the Fort Smith Commercial College. Courses were offered in typing, penmanship, mathematics, shorthand, bookkeeping, and correspondence. The college was at Fifth and Main Streets. George Neale Jr. took over for his father, George Neale Sr., who died in 1917. This photograph was taken around 1920. (Fort Smith Public Library Genealogy Department Postcard Collection.)

This 1909 postcard looks north on Fifteenth Street, with St. Edward's Infirmary on the left. This structure was built in 1905 and remodeled in 1940. These houses are directly east of Immaculate Conception Church, St. Anne's Convent, the current Immaculate Conception Church gymnasium, and the former St. Edward's Hospital building, which now serves as an apartment building for senior citizens. (Fort Smith Museum of History.)

This view of North Fifteenth Street shows progress and prosperity, as happy, well-dressed couples stroll through affluent neighborhoods of large homes and drive expensive automobiles on brick-paved streets. Fort Smith began paving its streets in 1914. (Fort Smith Museum of History.)

Garrison Avenue began to have more automobile traffic through the 1920s, as the population increased from 11,311 in 1890 to over 31,000 by 1930. This view to the east on Garrison shows the Douglas European Hotel on the left, the Hotel Main on the right, Nathan Clothing Store, at least two cafés, three banks, and, at the far left end, the Goldman Hotel. (Fort Smith Museum of History.)

This 1908 view to the east of Garrison Avenue shows the renovated Fort Smith High School on the left, with its castle-like spires, and the First Baptist Church of Fort Smith across the street. (Fort Smith Museum of History.)

D.J. Young brought Anheuser-Busch to Fort Smith in 1888 and was president of the Arkansas Refining Company. Ben Cravens was an attorney and the US congressman for the Western District of Arkansas in the early 1900s and again in the 1930s. Louis Berdelle worked in many businesses in Fort Smith including designing refrigeration techniques for meatpacking plants. Charles Jewett, the manager of the refinery, received a papal Knight of St. Gregory honor and, two years later, received a second honor, the Grand Cross Knight of the Holy Sepulcher, for his charity work in the Fort Smith area for more than 40 years. (Fort Smith National Historic Site Postcard Collection.)

D.J. Young's unique home is seen here on West Dodson Avenue between what are now Wheeler and Towson Avenues. Young's Fort Smith Steam Bottling Works began distributing Anheuser-Busch products in 1888, making it one of the oldest distributors of the St. Louis company's products in the nation. Anheuser-Busch continues to this day in Fort Smith as Belle Point Beverages, Inc. Young's plant also produced ginger ale and other types of beverages, including Coca-Cola, which was sold as early as 1894. By 1895, J.W. and Robert Meek had bought Young's company, moved it to South Second Street and Rogers Avenue, and renamed it J.W. & Robert Meek Manufacturing Confectioners and the Fort Smith Steam Bottling Works. The Meek family continues to distribute Coca-Cola in Fort Smith. (Fort Smith Public Library Genealogy Department Postcard Collection.)

This 1920s postcard looks west on Garrison Avenue and illustrates the need for traffic signals as trolley cars and automobiles traverse the wide street. The new Free Bridge crossing over into Oklahoma at the far end of the photograph was opened in 1922 for the nearly 28,000 residents of Fort Smith. (Fort Smith Museum of History.)

The Goldman Hotel is seen here around 1915. Will Rogers, Dizzy Dean, Buster Brown—and his dog, Tige—Eleanor Roosevelt, Bob Burns, Harry Truman, Elvis Presley, and others all stayed in this landmark hotel. (Fort Smith Public Library Genealogy Department Postcard Collection.)

The Sebastian Hotel Company began building this hotel in 1908 but ran into money troubles. Jacob Goldman, a St. Louis-based cotton broker who lived in Fort Smith, financed the $300,000 for the completion of two wings on North Thirteenth Street in 1910–1911. A third wing was added in 1929. For many, the Goldman was the place to be for leisure or business from 1910 into the 1940s, when motels and various new modes of transportation eclipsed the thrill of extended stays in grand hotels. (Stan Kujawa collection.)

John England was the manager of the Goldman Hotel in 1930 and offered KFPW radio, run by Jimmy Barry, the top floor. The radio station broadcast nightly dances with a house band, Eddie Simon's 10-piece orchestra. Many fraternal organizations utilized the large facilities and the unique service of the elaborate dining halls. Well-dressed waiters, bellhops, and other personnel provided a special place for residents and travelers alike. Guests could prepare for business with a shoe shine and a shave or unwind in the lobby or bookmaking rooms, playing dice, placing bets, or catching up with the latest news. Between 1945 and 1974, as Garrison Avenue evolved and Fort Smith's retail center moved west and south, hotels such as the Goldman became hulking shells of their former glory. The hotel closed in 1974 and was demolished in 1995. (Stan Kujawa collection.)

The Hotel Main was constructed in 1884 by Dr. J.H.T. Main for about $100,000. This German-printed postcard from the early 1900s provides an account of the life of many of the Fort Smith travelers who utilized the numerous hotels on Garrison Avenue. It reads, "Kansas City Mo. to-night Muscogee [sic] I.T. Sunday c/o Turner Hotel-Very busy-yours, Frank." Kansas City, Missouri, is nearly 270 miles from Muskogee, Oklahoma, which is about 75 miles from Fort Smith. This traveler, "Frank," likely took the Kansas City Southern Railway route for his journey. This structure was demolished in 1949. (Stan Kujawa collection.)

This 1933 view of Garrison Avenue looks to the east from Fifth Street and reveals the lack of streetcars and the addition of asphalt, which covered the original brick-paved streets. Henry Bollinger's music store, which offered piano tuning and repair and was the "sole agent for Brunswick Phonograph Records" in 1920, is on the left, at 423 Garrison Avenue. The Ward Hotel is also seen on the left, across from the First National Bank of Fort Smith. (Fort Smith Museum of History.)

The Ward Hotel, more than 140 feet tall, opened in 1929 with 165 rooms. According to historian Ben Boulden, Fort Smith's furniture industry included Fort Smith Couch and Bedding Co., Mitchell and Mitchell, Ballman-Cummings Furniture Co., Fort Smith Chair Co., and Fort Smith Folding Bed and Table Co. These local companies provided the furniture for the distinctive designs of each room in the hotel. The Ward suffered the same fate as many Garrison Avenue businesses and other hotels, closing in the 1970s. Sacred Grounds Coffee is in the former café attached to the Ward Hotel, while various businesses, including real estate offices, contractors, attorneys, and others continue to lease space within the impressive building. The coffee shop, lobby, and sidewalk areas were used in promotional photographs for a 2004 Roland (Oklahoma) High School musical production of *The 1940s Radio Hour.* (Fort Smith Museum of History.)

The Ward Hotel was advertised as "Fort Smith's newest and finest," with 200 rooms (from a 1950s update) and rates of "$2.00 and up." Additionally, the hotel offered "circulating ice water, ceiling fans," an "air-conditioned coffee shop," and free parking. This card was made by MWM Color Litho in Aurora, Missouri. (Goff Collection, Pebley Center, University of Arkansas-Fort Smith Boreham Library.)

The Southern Hotel was built in 1889 on North Sixth Street, off of Garrison Avenue. This 1950s postcard shows the special amenities of the popular grill, one of Fort Smith's numerous cafeterias, and a modern lobby. Also known as the Carlton Hotel, the building housed an Army recruiting office and the Palace Drug Store in later years. (Stan Kujawa collection.)

Postcards such as this one from the early 1900s represent the humorously designed postcards of the time. Many cards in this pennant style were made for "insert town name here" cards from 1912 to 1920. Pictures and captions were usually stock and could be used for locations from London to San Francisco and all points in between. (Stan Kujawa collection.)

Novelty postcards such as this one suggest that Fort Smith residents appreciated their city. It also illustrates the "wish you were here" sentiment of many postcards. The whimsical note says, "You may sing of the castles in sunny Spain and its soft and balmy air, But it tempts me not, for I love this spot, And would rather be here than there." (Stan Kujawa collection.)

This 1917 novelty postcard is one of a kind. The message has multiple meanings: the little cowboy recalls Fort Smith's history as a frontier town and conjures images of early film stars such as Lash LaRue and Tom Mix, but the caption could be interpreted as meaning there is not enough to do in this particular place, since the cowboy appears bored. (Stan Kujawa collection.)

The 1910-era card below seeks to draw visitors through Fort Smith's history and show off its deluxe accommodations and economic prosperity. At the time, slightly more than 23,000 people lived in Fort Smith. Postcards showing a thriving Garrison Avenue and ties to the historical past helped draw business, tourism, and appreciation to Fort Smith, as they still do today. (Stan Kujawa collection.)

Fort Smith's history of "Hell on the Border" law and order is glossed over in this postcard with the new century's technological advances, such as the electric trolley, and the new opportunities in the area. The card seeks to entice investors, merchants, and travelers to the border city in the early 1900s. (Stan Kujawa collection.)

Showcased in the early-1900s postcard below are the powerful cotton compress—one of the most productive in the nation—the Grand Opera House on Garrison Avenue, and the Missouri Pacific Railroad Bridge. The 1,100-seat Grand Opera House opened in 1888 at Fifth Street and Garrison Avenue. The Missouri Pacific Railroad was one of several to run lines through Fort Smith for agricultural products, natural resources, and other goods. (Stan Kujawa collection.)

This 1922 postcard shows the Free Bridge, which leads from Garrison Avenue to Oklahoma. The bridge served as a safe pedestrian crossing for day and evening travelers and a way westward for the new automobiles. The bridge helped increase the quality of life and the economic development in many Oklahoma communities across the river as well as helping Fort Smith to grow. This bridge was replaced in the 1970s during the expansion of the Arkansas River Navigation System. (Fort Smith National Historic Site Postcard Collection.)

This bridge opened on May 11, 1922, as the former Albert Pike Highway Free Bridge, heading west across the river from Garrison Avenue. The highway is no longer named after Pike, but Fort Smith recognized his contributions to the area by naming a local street and grade school after him. The bridge is now known as the J. Fred Patton Bridge, after the local historian, who devoted much of his life to studying Fort Smith's unique history. A 1996 tornado annihilated many nearby buildings. In recent years, after some renovation, the Park at West End was built to the north of the bridge, offering a special place for folks of all ages to enjoy a 1935 Ferris wheel, a historical carousel, and the Boomerang Café, a local restaurant housed in a Pullman car. (Fort Smith Public Library Genealogy Department Postcard Collection.)

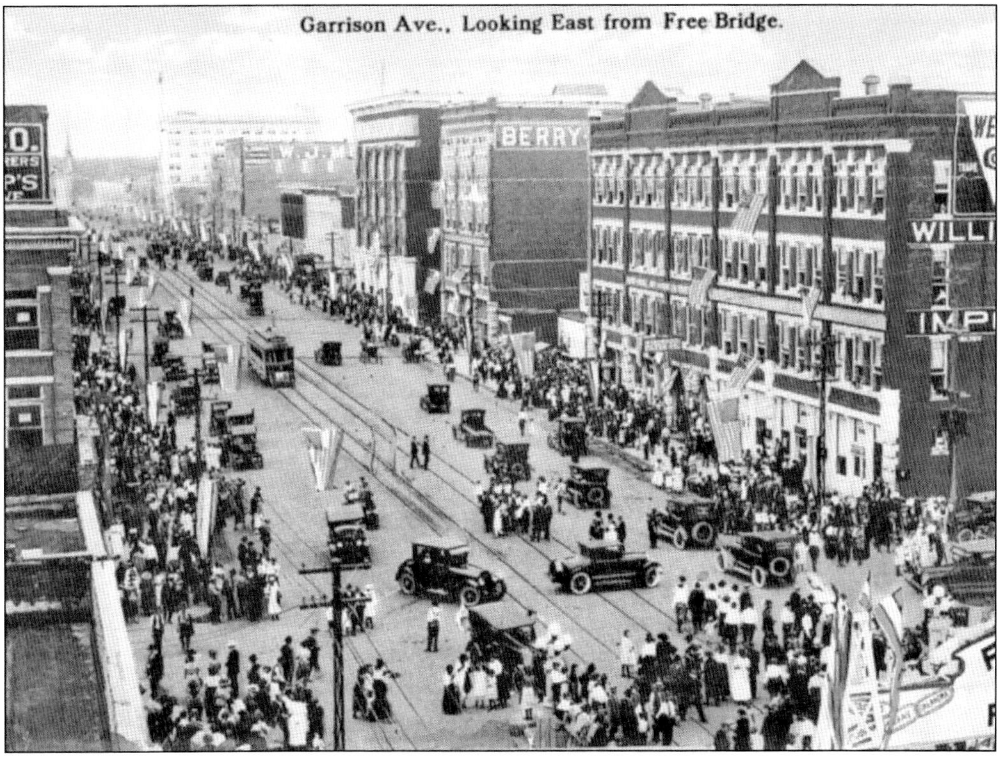

The opening of the 3,168-foot Free Bridge across the Arkansas River on May 11, 1922, is seen above in this eastern view of Garrison Avenue. The bridge was often referred to as the "Million Dollar Free Bridge." The governors of Arkansas and Oklahoma attended the ceremonies, as did more than 25,000 people, including 80 former US marshals. There were 10 bands, 8 Army planes, fireworks, and an evening electric exposition on Garrison Avenue. (Fort Smith Museum of History.)

The Wide Awake Café at 522 Garrison Avenue in Fort Smith is seen in this postcard from around 1920. The Ward Hotel and Sacred Grounds Coffee are now on the approximate spot where the café stood. (Fort Smith National Historic Site Postcard Collection.)

This 1909 postcard looking west on Garrison Avenue at night profiles how progressive electricity was in Fort Smith. The passing electric trolley can be seen, along with streetlamps and various automobiles, including an early Ford to the right. The Grand Opera House is to the left. (Fort Smith Chamber of Commerce.)

In this view looking east in 1918, dapper men and fashionable ladies make their way across the broad Garrison Avenue. The trolley lines are clearly visible in the center of the street. (Fort Smith Museum of History.)

Electric Park is seen here at night in 1909. The hundreds of twinkling lights awaiting visitors to Fort Smith's Electric Park created quite a spectacle. The park was originally created to provide more trolley business after normal work hours and on weekends. (Fort Smith Public Library Genealogy Department Postcard Collection.)

This moving-company postcard from the early 1900s encourages visitors to become residents and to use Merchant's Transfer Co. trucks. (Stan Kujawa collection.)

Fort Smith's Country Club, on Midland Boulevard, is seen here in 1904. It offered "2,398 yards of golf from the longest tees for a par of 35. The course rating is 70.0 and it has a slope rating of 113." Fort Smith's is the second-oldest public golf course west of the Mississippi. It was the first of the city's five golf courses, which include the Golf Links of Fort Smith, Hardscrabble Country Club, Ben Geren Public Golf Course, and Fianna Hills Country Club. Additionally, the First Tee of Fort Smith offers year-round instruction for toddlers, children, and teens and a small course for classes, local school use, and special events. (Fort Smith Public Library Genealogy Department Postcard Collection.)

The Lake Fort Smith Spillway near Mountainburg, Arkansas, was formed from erosion when the reservoir for Fort Smith's drinking water was created in 1936 by the WPA and the Civilian Conservation Corps (CCC). This feature was a favorite recreation spot for many until 2005, when the spillway was covered as part of renovations to Lake Fort Smith State Park. Trails, a marina, swimming, and camping are still offered. (Fort Smith Museum of History.)

This 1930s aerial view of Lake Fort Smith shows the original CCC and WPA dam, lake, and recreation areas. The area was enlarged in 2005, and the camping areas were moved. (Fort Smith Museum of History.)

This 1930s postcard is a version of the earlier photograph by Bob McCann of the Lake Fort Smith spillway near Mountainburg, Arkansas. (Fort Smith Museum of History.)

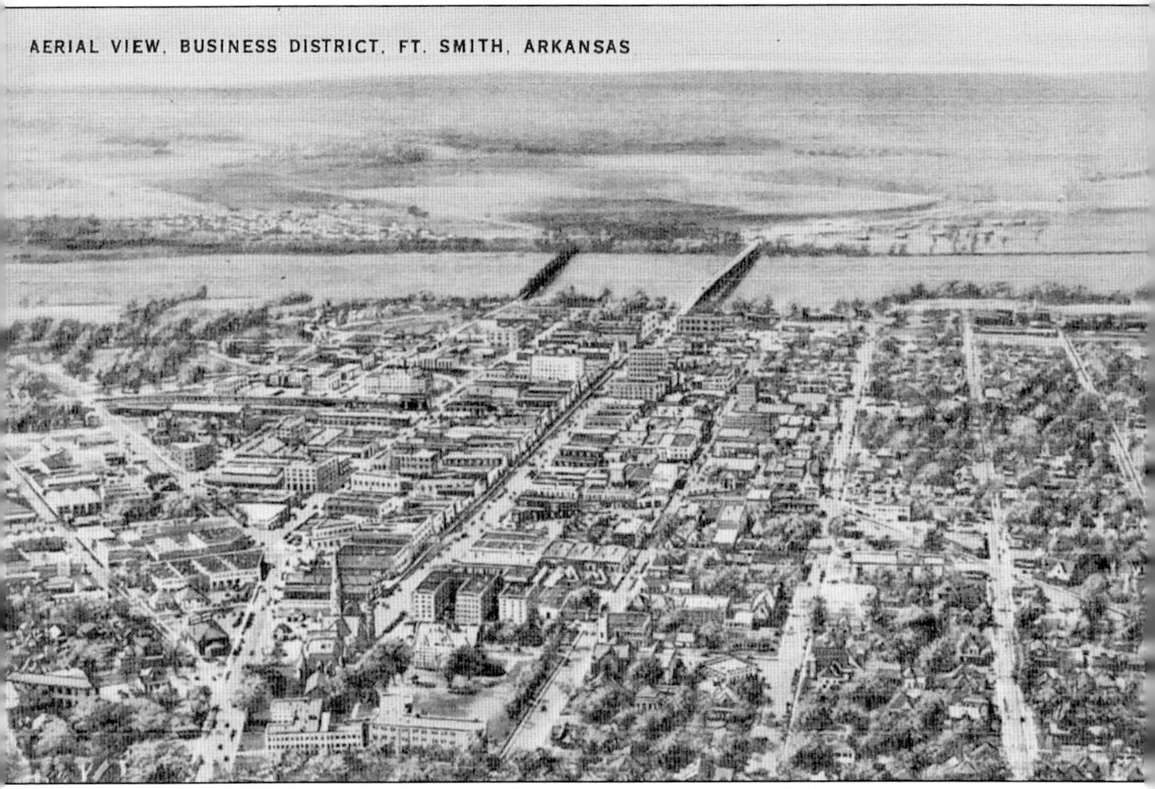

This postcard shows an aerial view of downtown Fort Smith in 1938. The new courthouses on Sixth Street are clearly visible, as are other large landmarks such as the three-wing Goldman Hotel and the Immaculate Conception Church, at the head of Garrison Avenue. (Fort Smith Museum of History.)

This building was dedicated in 1924 by a "community of Benedictine Sisters in Fort Smith, Arkansas," founded in 1879. It currently houses the combined Benedictine and Sisters of Mercy orders, who still have retreats and continue to work on counseling and service to the poor through Project Compassion. The former academy on the same grounds houses Trinity Junior High School. (Fort Smith Museum of History.)

Garrison Avenue is seen here in this 1940s souvenir postcard package promoting local businesses and resources. The Joie Theatre, which burned in 1953, is on the left, along with a Walgreen Drugs. Recently been renovated and sold, the Arcade (right), at 823 Garrison Avenue, was home to Davis Furniture for many decades. The Woolworth's, Dixie Shoes, and the Ward Hotel are all seen here as well. All three closed in the 1970s. (Fort Smith Museum of History.)

This is a 1944 view of St. Edward's Hospital on Rogers Avenue. St. Edward's was one of many early hospitals in the downtown area. In the 1940s and 1950s, this facility contributed to the influx of neighborhood businesses, including drugstores, florists, insurance offices, and nearby gas stations, all serving hospital employees, visitors, and patients. Some of these businesses remain today, but as St. Edward's moved west and Spark's Hospital grew to the south, many vacated this area of Rogers Avenue near Garrison Avenue. (Fort Smith Museum of History.)

Clear Creek, in the Ozarks north of Fort Smith toward Mountainburg, is seen here from US Highway 71. In 1928, Crawford County received a bridge, which was then refurbished in the 1950s. Clear Creek continues to offer visitors a scenic route and many opportunities to enjoy the outdoors, including hiking trails, camping, and rafting. River stops included historic Chester, Winslow, and Mountainburg. (Fort Smith Museum of History.)

Springtime in the Ozarks is seen in this 1944 postcard showing the view from near White Rock Mountain, north of Fort Smith. White Rock Mountain, part of the Boston Mountains in Northwest Arkansas, offers a lodge, cabins, trails, and camping as part of the Ozark National Forest region. White Rock is north from Interstate 40 near Mulberry, on Arkansas Highway 215 in the Shores Lake Recreation Area. (Fort Smith Museum of History.)

The dam at Devil's Den State Park, north of Fort Smith near Mountainburg, is seen in this 1944 promotional postcard. This park was built by the WPA and the CCC in the 1930s. In addition to swimming areas, the park also includes hiking trails, caves, camping, and cabin rentals. (Fort Smith Museum of History.)

Old Fort Smith, also known as the "Second Fort Smith," was a postcard favorite. W.L. Friend bought the image in 1908 and sold many versions of it in his Garrison Avenue retail store. This is a version of the image sold in the 1944 series. (Fort Smith Museum of History.)

"Greetings from Fort Smith" proclaims this 1944 souvenir packet, which uses a common format for postcards in the 1940s and 1950s. The font and colors were used by many companies nationwide as more people crossed the nation on Route 66 and, eventually, on the Interstate Highway System developed in the 1950s. (Fort Smith Museum of History.)

Before the 1990s, when the Bobby Hopper Tunnel near Winslow was completed and other improvements were made to Interstate 540, all traffic north of Fort Smith went through various towns such as Mountainburg on US Highway 71. These roads are still an attractive option when travelers are searching for scenic beauty and peace away from the rush of the interstate crowd. Many interesting roadside attractions and distinctive towns dot the forgotten highway systems of Northwest Arkansas. (Fort Smith Museum of History.)

The "grotto" on the convent grounds, seen here as part of the 1944 packet of Fort Smith souvenir postcards, was created from the remains of Pres. Zachary Taylor's home after an 1870s fire. President Taylor was a commander of Fort Smith prior to his Mexican War service and his presidency. (Fort Smith Museum of History.)

The 1937 city hall and county courthouse building (below) adorns the outside envelope of the Fort Smith souvenir postcard package from 1944. The prominent Confederate soldier monument reflects the area's promotion of its heritage. Built by the Monumental Cut Stone Company, the statue was placed on the courthouse grounds by the area's Confederate veterans and dedicated on September 10, 1903. Originally, this statue was to be placed in the Fort Smith National Cemetery, but then US secretary of state John Hay objected to the "Lest We Forget" portion of the epitaph. Hay served as Abraham Lincoln's secretary and was present when Lincoln died. For many, even as late as 1903, the wounds of the Civil War had yet to heal. (Fort Smith Museum of History.)

This highway scene invites travelers to follow the road to Fort Smith. This was the front of the inside cover of the 1944 Fort Smith souvenir postcard packet. The freedom of the open road enticed many in the 1940s and 1950s, as new highways and a postwar economy fostered national growth and focused attention on natural resources. (Fort Smith Museum of History.)

The post headquarters for Camp Chaffee (later Fort Chaffee), near Barling, Arkansas, are seen here. Chaffee was dedicated in 1940. The first 600 troops of the 6th Armored Division arrived in 1942. Many troops from Camp Chaffee assisted flood victims in Fort Smith and Van Buren in May 1943, when more than 250 people lost their homes and needed shelter. (Fort Smith Museum of History.)

This service club, seen in this 1943 postcard of Camp Chaffee, was one of two service clubs at the camp. Chaffee hosted the 5th Armored or "Victory" Division, and soldiers used these buildings for recreation and relaxation. (Fort Smith Museum of History.)

This late-1950s postcard shows troops going into one of the many chapels at Fort Chaffee. Many who served at Chaffee decided to marry local girls in some of these on-base chapels during their time or as they were leaving the Army. Fort Chaffee is responsible for bringing not only economic development and military training grounds to the area, but also for building communities, as many men stayed in Fort Smith after their enlistments. (Fort Smith Museum of History.)

The post headquarters at Chaffee are seen here in the 1950s. Fort Chaffee was named after Maj. Gen. Adna Chaffee in the 1940s. The large installation has been the site of mobile artillery training, mechanized troop schools, a camp for German prisoners of war during World War II, and refugee camps for Vietnamese and Cuban immigrants in the 1970s and 1980s. In 2005, victims of Hurricane Katrina were also housed at Fort Chaffee. The Arkansas National Guard currently uses 66,000 acres for training purposes, and the Chaffee Crossing area is revitalizing the local economy with new businesses, houses, and the Janet Huckabee River Valley Nature Center, among other attractions. (Fort Smith Museum of History.)

William Orlando Darby, the founder of the Army Rangers, was born on February 9, 1911, in Fort Smith. Darby became the youngest commission general in the army during World War II. He received mortal wounds during operations in northern Italy on April 30, 1945, and is buried in the Fort Smith National Cemetery. (Fort Smith Museum of History.)

The Bailey residence on Lexington Avenue is seen above in 1914. The home of Dr. W.W. Bailey, it was originally built in 1887. Bailey's father, Dr. Joseph H. Bailey, was an Army surgeon at Fort Gibson who married Lillie Main, whose father, Dr. J.H.T. Main, owned the Main Hotel on Garrison Avenue. It is believed that the Bailey Hill Reservoir now covers the site of this home, off of S Street. (Stan Kujawa collection.)

The C.W.L. Armour residence is at right. Armour was a county commissioner for a time and was instrumental in the building of the courthouse in Van Buren, which still stands today. Armour was also a Fort Smith Library public trustee and was elected president of the Arkansas Library Association in 1911. (Stan Kujawa collection.)

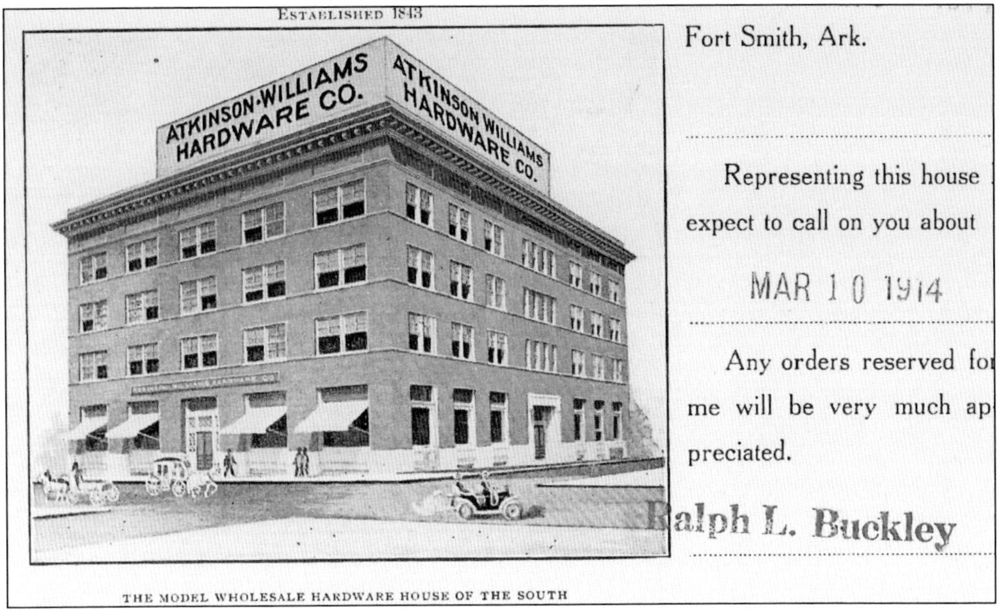

The Atkinson-Williams Hardware Building is seen here in 1914. The building is now the home of the Fort Smith Museum of History, at 320 Rogers Avenue. Built in 1906, it was placed on the National Register of Historic Places in 1979. The Fort Smith Museum of History offers many unique exhibits, including a working 1920s drugstore; special collections showing the region's political, social, and economic evolution with prehistoric artifacts and pioneer clothing; an 1800s woodworking shop; and much more—leading all the way to the present day. (Stan Kujawa collection.)

The interior of Fort Smith's Majestic Theatre is seen here in the 1920s. The screen is set, the piano is down center, and all the seats are waiting for eager customers to see the latest talkie. (Stan Kujawa collection.)

Weldon, Williams, and Lick was formed in 1898 by Oliver D. "Bud" Weldon, George T. Williams, and Chauncey A. Lick. Originally, the company printed various items, including the *Fort Smith Elevator* newspaper and various other print jobs. The company was first located where Regions Bank is today on Garrison Avenue. Early print jobs included printing tickets for the Barnum and Bailey Circus and St. Louis Cardinals games. Today, it continues to print various types of tickets, permits, decals, armbands, and souvenirs for customers throughout the world, including state and local governments, colleges and universities, and major ticket outlets. The company still operates in Fort Smith at 711 North A Street. (Stan Kujawa collection.)

The Kansas City Southern Railway Bridge at the mouth of the Poteau River near Belle Point is seen in this 1940s postcard. The bridge was constructed in 1891 and the Kansas City, Fort Smith & Southern Railway began in 1886. By 1903, lines existed from Fort Smith to Coal Creek and to Guthrie, Oklahoma, through Spiro, Oklahoma. The Missouri-Kansas-Texas Railroad Company (MKT, or the Katy) was also influential in opening rail traffic from Oklahoma City to Joplin, Missouri, and down to the Gulf of Mexico through Muskogee, Oklahoma, and Fort Smith. (Fort Smith Museum of History.)

The flood of May 1943 forced more than 250 residents to abandon their homes. Troops from Fort Chaffee, then Camp Chaffee, assisted the American Red Cross with relief efforts; three soldiers drowned in the effort. The Army constructed a pontoon bridge between Fort Smith and Van Buren, and hundreds of people helped to fill sandbags. The Arkansas River Navigation System, Lock and Dam 13, and Kerr Dam near Sallisaw, Oklahoma, all assisted in controlling the rising Arkansas River. (Fort Smith Museum of History.)

The 1912 Van Buren–Fort Smith train bridge was in great peril during the May 1943 flood. This image and many others were donated by former private first class Raymond W. Schmidt of Battery A, 14th Armored Division, commanded by Maj. Gen. Vernon J. Pritchard. The 1943 flood hastened new construction, as the bridge's south end was damaged and the north end was lost. The rebuilding of the bridge on the original 1885 pilings continued into the 1970s. The bridge is still in use today. (Fort Smith Museum of History.)

The 1891 Frisco and Kansas City Southern Bridge near Belle Point was weighed down with loaded train cars to keep it from washing away during the spring of 1943. The Kansas City Southern Railway established service to Monett, Missouri, from Fort Smith in the 1880s, and continues to haul freight today. Passenger service discontinued out of Fort Smith in the 1960s. (Fort Smith Museum of History.)

This early-1900s postcard shows the importance of transportation in Fort Smith since the 1800s. Companies in Fort Smith and Springfield, Missouri, were responsible for making many of the wagons that settled the western states. (Stan Kujawa collection.)

Begun in 1939, the Fort Smith Municipal Airport, seen here in the 1950s, was the first airport in the area and originally had sod runways. Now the Fort Smith Regional Airport, the facility handles freight, small planes, and the 188th Air National Guard Fighter Wing, which has been in Fort Smith since 1954. It also offers scheduled passenger service. The airport has also been the sight of many popular air shows in recent years. A new terminal was completed in 2002. (Stan Kujawa collection.)

Neumeier's Chickuisine is one of the many restaurant ventures of the Neumeier family. Neumeier's Rib Room and Papa's Pub and Pizzeria have both operated successfully on Garrison Avenue for many years. The Rib Room offers good food and an outdoor venue for touring musicians, while Papa's has become one Garrison's most popular gathering places for, as the reverse indicates, "music, laughter, conversation, and gentlemanly sporting events." This Chickuisine postcard is an example of restaurant advertising in the 1950s. (Fort Smith Museum of History.)

Luby's Cafeteria is one of many cafeterias that served the citizens of Fort Smith. This location is no longer in business, but it is near the current location of Logan's Roadhouse off of Interstate 540 and Rogers Avenue. Postcards were used for advertising by many restaurants in the 1960s. Cafeterias offered a variety of dishes at an affordable price and appealed to many working families. The cafeteria appeals to the American sensibility of "bigger, better, faster, and more." (Fort Smith Chamber of Commerce.)

Downtown Garrison Avenue was in transition in the 1950s, as the postwar boom brought urban sprawl and the downtown areas of many cities begin to decline. Many of the largest hotels and once popular retail stores hung on into the 1980s or survived to today, but most faded out in the 1960s and 1970s. (Fort Smith Chamber of Commerce.)

This view of Free Bridge to the east shows the city going through another transition. This stylistic postcard depicts John Schaap and Sons Drug Co., which operated on Garrison Avenue for many years. The Vaughn-Schaap House on Sixth Street, built in the 1850s, housed the Fort Smith Art Museum for decades and is currently occupied by the office of US congressman Steve Womack. Oklahoma Transfer and Storage Company, on the right, organized in 1923 and became ABF Freight System, Inc., one of the nation's largest trucking companies. (Fort Smith Chamber of Commerce.)

Handy Dan's Pantry began doing business in Fort Smith under Council Manufacturing Company at 420 North Second Street in 1963. The company let patents expire in the 1980s on its interesting outdoor "merchandising cabinets, including compartments, one or more of which may be refrigerated," as the reverse of the card explains. (Stan Kujawa collection.)

John A. Stryker was a Western photographer from Kansas who created action souvenir postcard packets for the Fort Smith Rodeo and others. The Fort Smith Old Fort Days Rodeo has been a tradition since 1933. (Fort Smith Museum of History.)

This is another John A. Stryker photograph of a rodeo event in Fort Smith. These photographs were sold at the Fort Smith Rodeo and at other regional rodeos for $1 each in the 1940s and 1950s. Stryker began his photography career in Kansas, but some of his most famous work is of Fort Worth, Texas. (Fort Smith Museum of History.)

Stryker, whose packets were quite popular, never stopped taking pictures. Many of his works are in the National Cowboy & Western Heritage Museum in Oklahoma City. One story notes that, at age 80, he asked men in a fire ladder crew to hoist him in the air as high as they could, so he could "get the right shot." The firemen agreed, and Stryker got his photograph. (Fort Smith Museum of History.)

The Old Fort Days Rodeo was originally held at the fairgrounds and then at Andrew's Field before moving to what is now Kay Rodgers Park. The rodeo has been a major contributor to the cultural and economic stability of the region. The earliest official rodeos in Fort Smith had to work around the schedule of a minor-league St. Louis Cardinals affiliate, which played at Andrew's Field. (Fort Smith Museum of History.)

Some of the events for the 2012 rodeo included a Miss Rodeo Old Fort Days Pageant, a signing contest, and a pony express relay. This 1940s packet showcases the heroes of past rodeos and the grit they showed. (Fort Smith Museum of History.)

The First National Bank of Fort Smith's 1958 addition created a drive-through and more office space. The bank, on the site of the Hotel Main, has evolved into the First Bank Corporation Financial Family, which includes the National Bank of Sallisaw; Citizens Bank and Trust Company in Van Buren; the acquisition and merger of River Valley Bank and Trust; First National Bank of Rogers, a division of the First National Bank of Fort Smith formerly known as the Bank of Rogers; Brown-Hiller-Clark and Associates; and Realty Appraisals, Inc. (Fort Smith Chamber of Commerce.)

The Fort Smith Chamber of Commerce building is seen here in the 1960s. The building now houses Landry's Cajun Restaurant, and the chamber offices are across the street. (Fort Smith Chamber of Commerce.)

Sparks Hospital is seen here in a promotional postcard from the chamber of commerce in the 1930s. Sparks was one of the first hospitals in Arkansas to offer a hospital-based fitness center, the Marvin Altman Center. It also made major innovations in medical imaging and robot-assisted surgery. Additional progress in cardiac care and cancer treatment has brought patients and medical professionals to Fort Smith. (Fort Smith Museum of History.)

Andrew "Cap" Tilles, a St. Louis cotton broker with family in Fort Smith, donated the land for this park, named for his father, Louis Tilles, in 1925. This park is a favorite of many in the area around Grand Avenue and Thirty-seventh Street, with its tennis and basketball courts, pavilions, and wading pool. (Fort Smith Museum of History.)

Lion's Park is seen here as part of a packet of postcards organized by the Fort Smith Chamber of Commerce to promote tourism and to improve the city's quality of life. Lion's Park is now known as Forsgren Field and continues to serve the youth of the area as a baseball field for Fort Smith Church League Baseball and also the Boys and Girls Club. (Fort Smith Museum of History.)

B Street is still "one of the many beautiful residence streets in the city," as many of these homes still exist on B Street, north of the Immaculate Conception gymnasium and the Monsignor Galvan Parish Center. The brick home on the far right is now a business location, and the building to the south is under renovation. Many houses on this street are in the National Register of Historic Places. (Fort Smith Museum of History.)

This "old Southern House and Garden" could be the Vaughn-Schaap House, built in the 1850s, which was home to the Fort Smith Art Museum until recently. Fort Smith's Belle Grove District contains some of the oldest homes in the city, although other Victorian treasures can be found on May, Lecta, Park, Rogers, and Adelaide Avenues, Free Ferry Road, and other streets. (Fort Smith Museum of History.)

Parker Ward School was an elementary school in Fort Smith for many years. Over the years, it became too small and required updated heating, electrical, and other systems. In 2006, it was remodeled to increase office space and student development for the district. Recent programs have focused on literacy and language development. (Fort Smith Museum of History.)

Fentress Mortuary continues to serve the River Valley from North A Street in Fort Smith. The funeral home and residence was built by Oscar and Mae Fentress in 1931. (Stan Kujawa collection.)

Edward's Funeral Home has been at North Twelfth and B Streets since 1936. Delmar D. and Hazel Edwards founded Edwards Funeral Home in 1933. A 1939 fire destroyed the original structure, and a new building was constructed the following year. (Stan Kujawa collection.)

The Fort Smith Motel was similar to many motor inns or hideaway cottages that weary visitors could drive directly up to without the hassle of a full-service hotel. (Fort Smith Public Library Genealogy Department Postcard Collection.)

Midland Boulevard's Blackburn Court offered a quiet "fireproof" bungalow in which to rest from the highway and had no bellhop service to pay for, as at the Goldman downtown. Times were changing, and these motels were accessible, cheaper, and comfortable for most travelers. (Goff Collection, Pebley Center, University of Arkansas-Fort Smith Boreham Library.)

Terry's Motor Court is still operating on Midland Boulevard, just down the road from Kay Rodgers Park, although it has gone through some changes over the years. (Fort Smith Public Library Genealogy Department Postcard Collection.)

Scenes of lavish hotel lobbies, such as this 1910 depiction of the Hotel Main, were fading in the 1960s and 1970s, as business travelers and families opted for self-service rather than full-service hotels. The demise of railway passenger service in the 1960s also influenced the loss of business for the grand hotels in Fort Smith and elsewhere. Motels became more convenient and cheaper for tourists and businessmen and easier for owners to maintain. By 1974, many of the largest and most elaborate hotels on Garrison Avenue were in ruin, demolished, or losing out to urban sprawl. (Stan Kujawa collection.)

This 1956 aerial shot of the town looks from the Fort Smith National Cemetery toward the north, showing the trains at the old Union Station, which was demolished in the 1960s. (Fort Smith Chamber of Commerce.)

This aerial shot of downtown Fort Smith in 1943 reveals that more trees were in the area back then and the river was untamed. Additionally, residences in Coke Hill to the west and north of the Free Bridge are visible, as are landmarks such as Andrews Field, the onetime home of a St. Louis Cardinals' minor-league team. (Fort Smith Chamber of Commerce.)

This modern aerial shot of downtown is interesting to compare to earlier photographs due to the changes, especially on Garrison Avenue, since 1870. The 1960 census shows the population at 52,991, while the 2010 census figure is 86,209. (Stan Kujawa collection.)

Three

A City Looking Forward to the Past

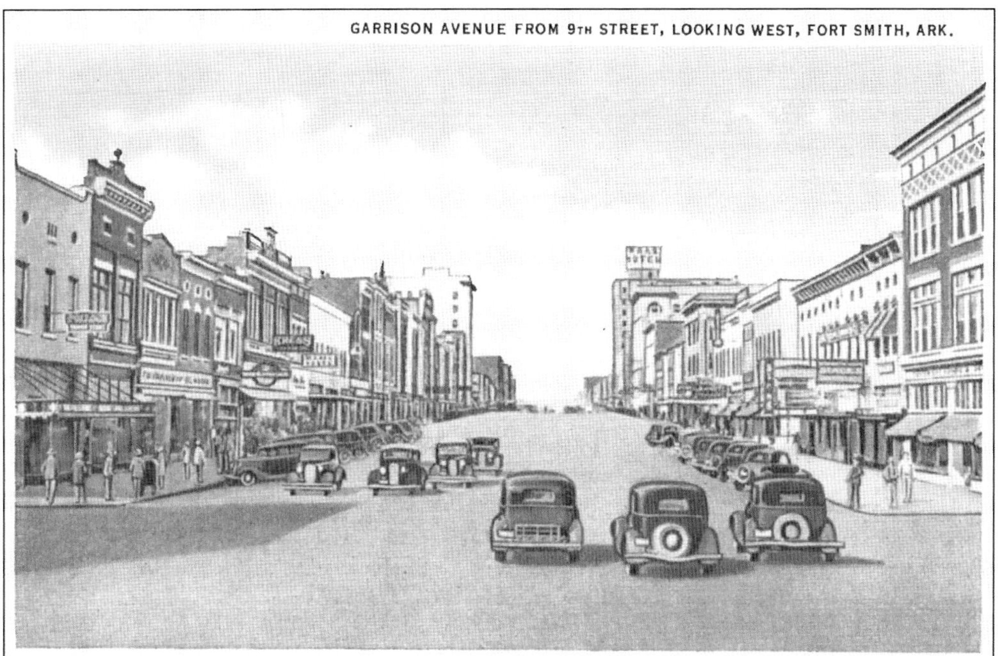

This view looks west from Ninth Street towards Garrison Avenue in 1942. Sears, Roebuck and Co. was on the right, across from the Kress store. The two tallest buildings on Garrison, the Ward Hotel building and First National Bank, remain today. Many of the other businesses either moved out in the 1960s and 1970s or were damaged by the 1996 tornado. (Fort Smith Public Library Genealogy Department Postcard Collection.)

This 1912 postcard advertises the Merchants National Bank and the Nakdiman Building. The Merchants building now houses the city offices. The Nakdiman Building was once the home of the Fort Smith Chamber of Commerce. Iser Nakdimen (spellings of the name differ), the founder of City National Bank and the Oklahoma and Arkansas Telephone Company, was a Russian-born immigrant who came to America as a youth. He is listed as a leader for Jewish relief efforts in 1921. Letters sent out that year to businessmen nationwide from the Chicago Conference on American Jewish Relief ask, "Shall we allow our fellow-Jews to sink back into chaos or shall we extend them the chance of becoming again the self-supporting, self-respecting, useful, productive Jews they formerly were?" (Fort Smith Public Library Genealogy Department Postcard Collection.)

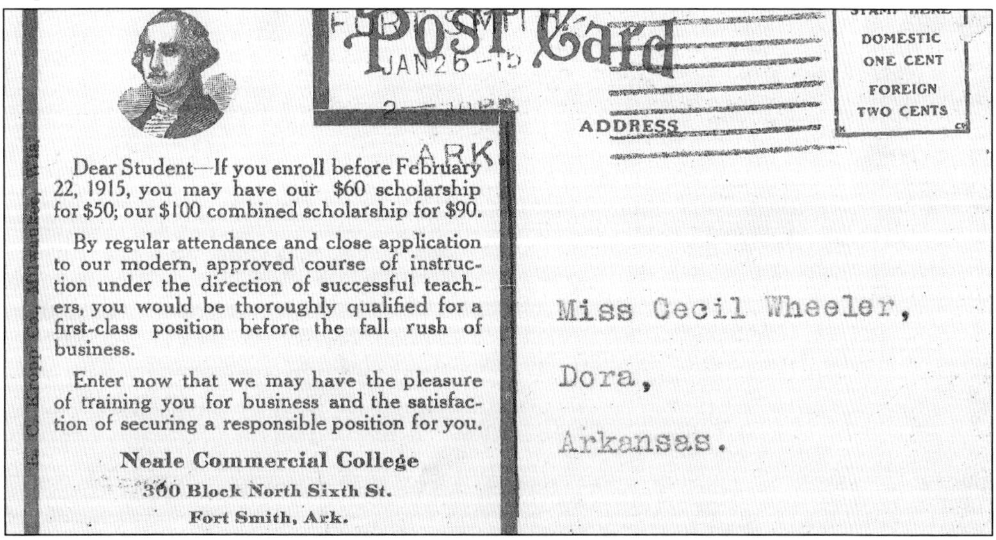

This 1915 advertisement for Neale Commercial College offers discounts on tuition and promises of employment upon graduation. Many enterprising young men took advantage of this scholarship opportunity to improve their futures and secure steady jobs. The aspirations and concerns of men and women of 1915 mirror those of today; Fort Smith's emphasis on local education has a long tradition. (Fort Smith Public Library Genealogy Department Postcard Collection.)

Fred G. Hicken operated a ticket brokerage in the Hotel Main in addition to a cigar and candy store. This advertisement promotes his exclusive affiliation with a New York candymaker. He died in 1912. (Stan Kujawa collection.)

A large crowd has gathered to hear Pres. Theodore Roosevelt speak on April 20, 1912, in front of the Frisco Passenger Railway depot and the Missouri Pacific freight depot at the western end of Garrison Avenue. The Frisco building, on the left, with the column, now holds the offices for the National US Marshals Museum. Garrison Avenue appears to be crowded to Fourth Street, as many of the 23,975 residents turned out to hear the speech. (Fort Smith Chamber of Commerce.)

Theodore Roosevelt (center, with right arm outstretched) did not seek a third term in 1908. In 1912, after his handpicked Republican successor, William Howard Taft, failed to adhere to Roosevelt's policies and Democrat Woodrow Wilson entered the race, Roosevelt became the candidate for the Progressive ("Bull Moose") Party. As one of the most successful third-party candidates in history, Roosevelt defeated Taft and Socialist candidate Eugene Debs but lost to Wilson. Over four million Americans gave Roosevelt 21 percent of the vote. He continued to lead an adventurous life until 1919, when he died at home after complications caused by malaria and a leg infection he contracted during a dangerous expedition in 1914 on the River of Doubt. (Fort Smith Chamber of Commerce.)

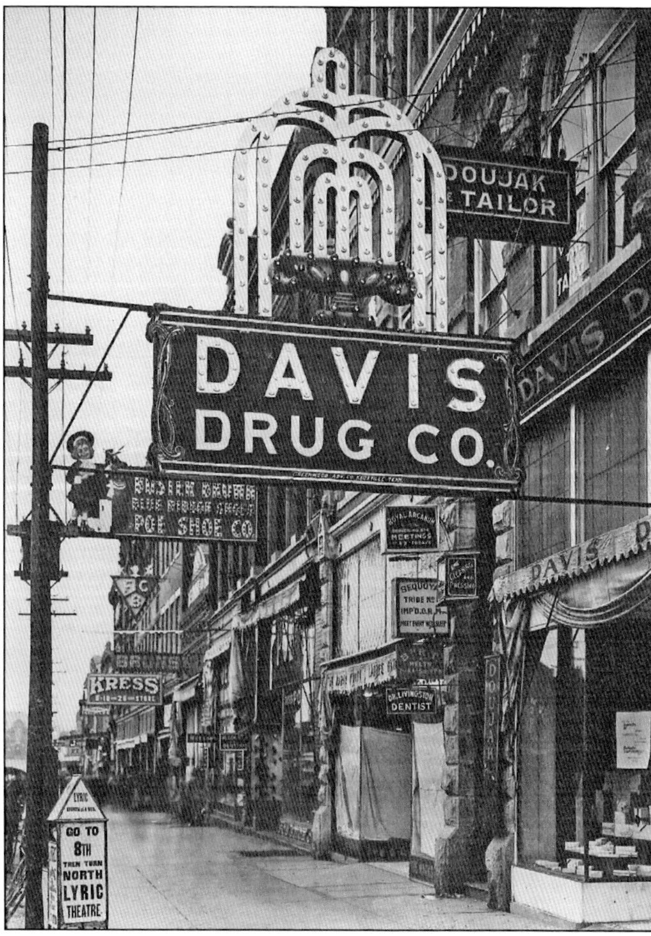

J.R. and J.P. Davis opened Davis Drug Store in 1911 at 716 Garrison Avenue. This shot clearly shows the Kress store sign and a Buster Brown Shoes sign. (Fort Smith Chamber of Commerce.)

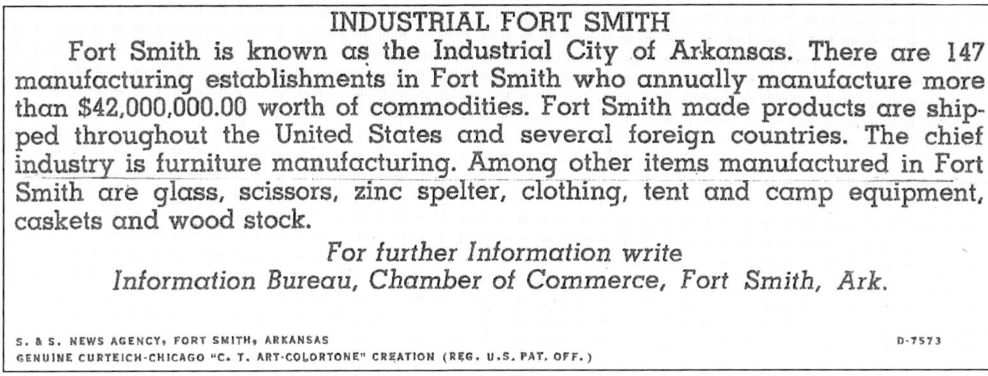

INDUSTRIAL FORT SMITH

Fort Smith is known as the Industrial City of Arkansas. There are 147 manufacturing establishments in Fort Smith who annually manufacture more than $42,000,000.00 worth of commodities. Fort Smith made products are shipped throughout the United States and several foreign countries. The chief industry is furniture manufacturing. Among other items manufactured in Fort Smith are glass, scissors, zinc spelter, clothing, tent and camp equipment, caskets and wood stock.

For further Information write
Information Bureau, Chamber of Commerce, Fort Smith, Ark.

S. & S. NEWS AGENCY, FORT SMITH, ARKANSAS D-7573
GENUINE CURTEICH-CHICAGO "C. T. ART-COLORTONE" CREATION (REG. U.S. PAT. OFF.)

In the 1940s, a souvenir postcard packet of Fort Smith was created to promote the city's virtues. Inside the cover and under the bright postcards of the "Old Fort," "The Grotto," and the Fort Smith High School, was a history of Fort Smith, which ended with the paragraph shown here. (Fort Smith Chamber of Commerce.)

This greenhouse was an integral part of the grounds at Electric Park for the Fort Smith Light and Traction Company in 1909. The Electric Park gardens were a draw for many visitors, and the unique plants were started and given special care in this building. The influence of botanical gardens in larger cities to the east and north of Fort Smith encouraged FSL&T to offer what were advertised as the most elaborate and well-kept gardens of any electric park in the nation. (Fort Smith Chamber of Commerce.)

This early-1900s postcard shows the Wholesale District on Garrison Avenue. Many of these buildings were completely torn apart during the 1996 tornado. On April 21, 1996, at 11:12 p.m., nearly the same exact time as the January 1898 tornado that killed 55 people, a major tornado caused millions of dollars of damage, killed two children, and wiped out many of the west end structures in this postcard. The archway and the front wall on the white and brick building at left remain, but the building, which was being renovated at the time, was demolished, along with many others. The Ross Pendergraft Park and the statue of Bass Reeves are now near the former site of the Lee Feed Store at left. (Fort Smith Chamber of Commerce.)

The Shipley Baking Company began in 1906 with Harry Shipley Sr. and Garvin Shipley. Until 1921, the Shipleys worked as partners with Thomas Edmonson at his bakery to learn the craft. The business was sold to Flowers Foods in 1998. Other bakers included the popular Von Hatten Bakery on I Street, which had one of the first Hobart mixers in the nation in 1919. Irish Maid Donuts on Towson and Rogers Avenues is a major part of the Fort Smith tradition of popular bakeries and baking companies. (Fort Smith Chamber of Commerce.)

Railroad workers pose with their handcarts and hammers at the ready as they lay track near Fort Smith in the 1890s. Fort Smith & Southern was organized in the 1880s as coal was being brought out from area mines. By 1920, the Missouri Pacific, MKT, and Frisco railroads brought men, materials, lines, passengers, freight, and money into Fort Smith. Rail traffic continues to export and import commodities for Fort Smith. However, the only passengers who ride these rails today are on short excursions to scenic destinations, as the glory days of sleeper trains in the United States ended in the 1960s. (Fort Smith Chamber of Commerce.)

FORT SMITH FACTS. City Directory Census, 1925, 37,012; Including Industrial Environs, 40,000; Tributary Trade Territory, 1,000,000; Mean Annual Temperature, 61 degrees; Average Annual Rainfall, 41 inches; Churches, all Denominations, 40; Schools, Public and Private, 18; Business Colleges, 2; $2,000,000 invested in Public School Property; 125 miles of Paved Streets; Five free bridges; Bank resources, $23,600,000; Annual check transactions (debits to individual accounts only), $154,000,000; Total property value, $66,000,000; Tax rate (state, county, city, school) .0322, (based on 50% assessed valuation); Adjacent fields contain more than Four Billion Tons of Coal; Fort Smith compresses annually 100,000 bales of cotton (300,000 bales within 100 miles, 80% to 90% high grade); 11,647 Persons engaged in gainful employment; 7,000 homes; 650 traveling salesmen live in Fort Smith; Per Capita Wealth, $2,062.00; Fort Smith is the largest distributing center in Arkansas; Fort Smith has 88 successful jobbing houses; Fort Smith's population consists of 85% Native White, 12% Negro, 3% Foreign Born; Fort Smith's illiteracy is considerably less than 3.4%, the smallest proportion of any City in the South; Fort Smith has more Railroads than any other City in Arkansas; The principal shops of the Frisco, Fort Smith & Western and Missouri Pacific are located in Fort Smith and Van Buren.

FORT SMITH, *"The Super-Power Center"—Natural Gas and Coal.*

Tourists, Homeseekers, Investors, Manufacturers and All Persons Interested are Invited to Write the

CHAMBER OF COMMERCE, FORT SMITH, ARKANSAS.

The last section of "Fort Smith Facts," from a 1925 postcard package from the Chamber of Commerce advocating the natural resources, demographics, and economic development opportunities for visitors, is seen here. Education, transportation, and a high quality of life are the focus of this section. (Fort Smith Museum of History.)

This 1923 view of the Free Bridge on Albert Pike Highway is from the north side of the bridge in Oklahoma looking toward Fort Smith. In the 1970s, this bridge was torn down to make way for improved navigation on the Arkansas River and because of neglect. (Goff Collection, Pebley Center, University of Arkansas-Fort Smith Boreham Library.)

Once the Fort Smith National Historical Site opened in 1964, postcards such as this one began to celebrate the earliest history of the area and the first fort. A few exhibits at the national historic site offer insight into the lives of Native Americans, but most focus on the fort. (Fort Smith Public Library Genealogy Department Postcard Collection.)

Fort Smith National Historic Site has helped increase tourism to the area. The excavation of the 1817 first Fort Smith was led by Clyde D. Dollar and Jackson W. Moore from 1958 to 1963. Roger Coleman and Jody Parrish have also contributed to a comprehensive understanding of the historical significance of the nearly 75-acre park grounds. This view at the original site of the first Fort Smith provides a vantage point across the Arkansas River into Oklahoma. (Fort Smith Public Library Genealogy Department Postcard Collection.)

Judge Isaac C. Parker's influence on Fort Smith continues to this day in the churches, schools, and hospitals he helped form. This postcard from the 1960s is evidence of a resurgence of interest in Parker's court, as tourism to Fort Smith increased during that decade. When Parker died at age 58 in 1896, a new era of appeal had come to the federal court system and many changes had occurred within Fort Smith. Parker will be remembered for his work ethic, his impressive number of cases, and his rigidity to the rule of law. (Fort Smith Public Library Genealogy Department Postcard Collection.)

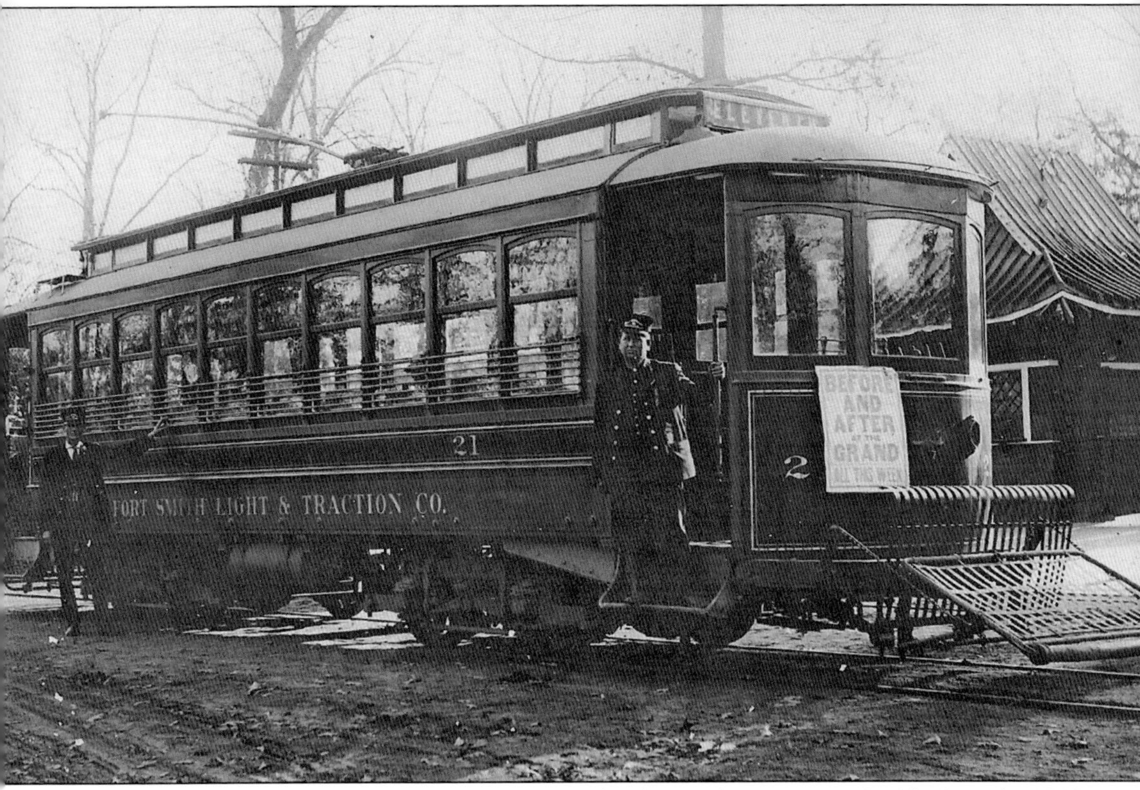

The Fort Smith Light and Traction Company has been reborn in Fort Smith since the 1990s, as a handful of trolleys take passengers on a ride back to the glory days of streetcars in the city, from 1894 to 1933. This particular car picked up at Eleventh Street and advertises a play at the Grand Opera House, *Before and After*. The no. 21 trolley is parked in front of Electric Park waiting to take passengers back to Eleventh Street. (Stan Kujawa collection.)

The little boy in this postcard is excited as he prepares to board for his 5¢ ride. Today, the Fort Smith Trolley Museum offers rides in downtown Fort Smith for under $2. Various historical stops are included on the tour, but passengers also have the option of riding without a tour. The refurbished trolleys are a unique draw for the downtown businesses and the museum district. The Travel Channel has showcased the trolley rides on several programs in recent years. (Stan Kujawa collection.)

The England Brothers Truck Line offices and distribution terminal at North Second Street are seen here around 1950. There were other terminals in Kansas City, St. Louis, Little Rock, and Memphis. As the second-largest city in Arkansas, Fort Smith has been an important transportation city for decades. Numerous companies have prospered because of trucking in the area since 1950, including Jones Truck Lines, Arkansas Best Freight, USA Truck, and Carman Trucking. (Fort Smith Public Library Genealogy Department Postcard Collection.)

This postcard looks east on Garrison Avenue west of Sixth Street in 1912. The Southern Hotel annex, which was at the corner of Sixth and Garrison, was demolished decades ago, while the Missouri Pacific Railroad building and Pape's Bookstore at left were replaced by the Ward Hotel. (Fort Smith Public Library Genealogy Department Postcard Collection.)

A man fishes at the confluence of the Poteau and Arkansas Rivers around 1910. Many Fort Smith area companies rely on river traffic and river products, including Arkhola Sand and Gravel, founded in 1840; fishing-lure maker PRADCO Fishing, founded in 1960; and the Arkansas Regional Intermodal Transportation Authority (RITA), which has announced a planned $15 million slack water harbor project. (Fort Smith Public Library Genealogy Department Postcard Collection.)

The Goldman Hotel's impressive main lobby, seen here in 1924, was an important meeting place for business and pleasure until the 1970s. Many of Fort Smith's major businessmen, including George Tilles, lived at the Goldman for a time. (Fort Smith Public Library Genealogy Department Postcard Collection.)

The Casino Building at Electric Park is decked out with bunting for a summer celebration in 1908. On the Fourth of July, Fort Smith has city fireworks displays hosted by the mayor at the downtown riverfront. (Fort Smith Public Library Genealogy Department Postcard Collection.)

The 1830s commissary building is one of the oldest buildings in Fort Smith. Judge Parker's office was in this building in the 1870s. For many years, it housed the Old Fort Museum, which later became known as the Fort Smith Museum of History. This 1960s image was used in many postcards sold at the Old Fort Museum. (Fort Smith Public Library Genealogy Department Postcard Collection.)

The Missouri Pacific freight depot served Fort Smith for decades. The Harry E. Kelley Park amphitheater, home to the annual Fort Smith Blues Festival and many other events, is now near the site of this building beside the Arkansas River. (Fort Smith Public Library Genealogy Department Postcard Collection.)

This building, at Third Street and Garrison Avenue, was once owned by William Fishback, the only governor of Arkansas from Fort Smith, who named it in honor of his wife, Adelaide Miller, who died in 1882. The 1871 building was the setting for many political activities, starting in the late 1800s. Adelaide Hall is home to the Varsity Sports Grill and the Adelaide Hall Ballroom. Fishback returned to Fort Smith after his term as governor, practiced law, and was buried in Oak Cemetery in 1903. (Fort Smith Chamber of Commerce.)

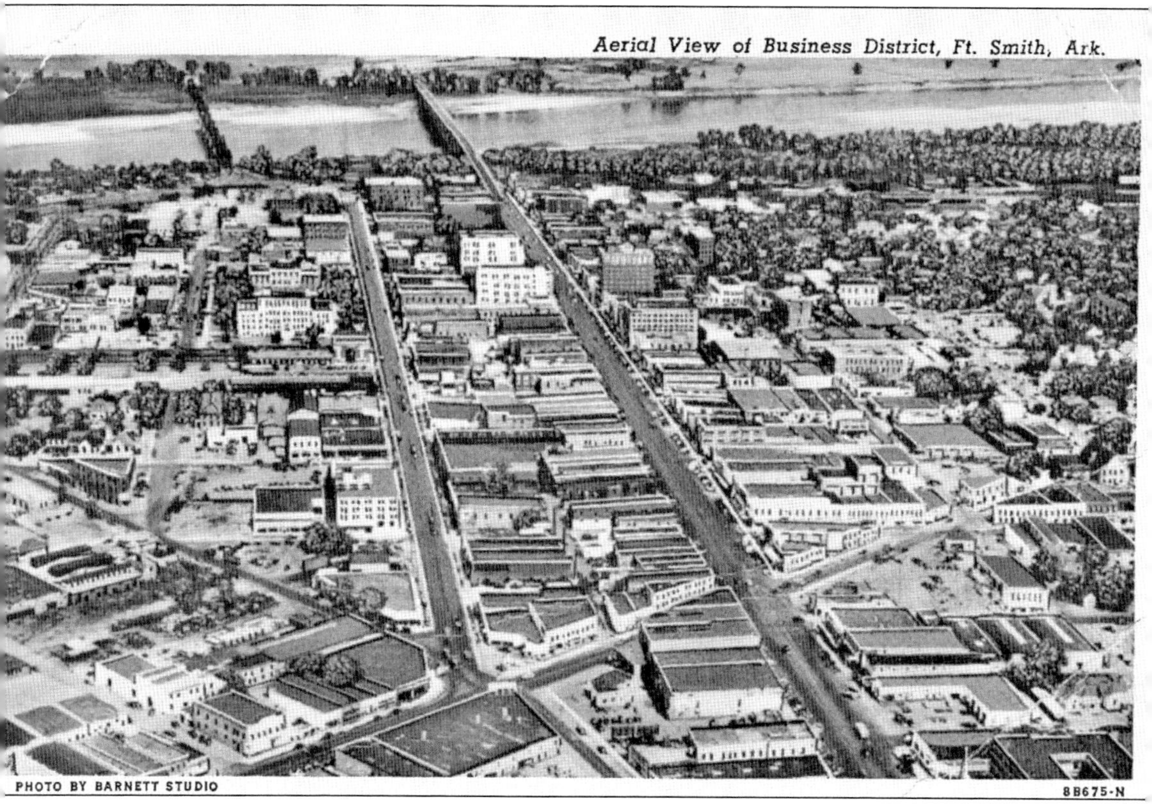

This aerial view shows the Fort Smith Business District in the 1940s. The Goldman Hotel is near the bottom of the postcard. The New Theatre, built within the Sparks Building on Tenth Street and Garrison Avenue in 1911, is seen here, as are the prosperous trucking and warehouse districts. It is rumored that tunnels existed under some businesses to the riverfront so that boats could unload their goods more quickly without blocking street traffic. The boats may have been delivering goods that were questionable under some laws, including the 1914 temperance laws. (Fort Smith Public Library Genealogy Department Postcard Collection.)

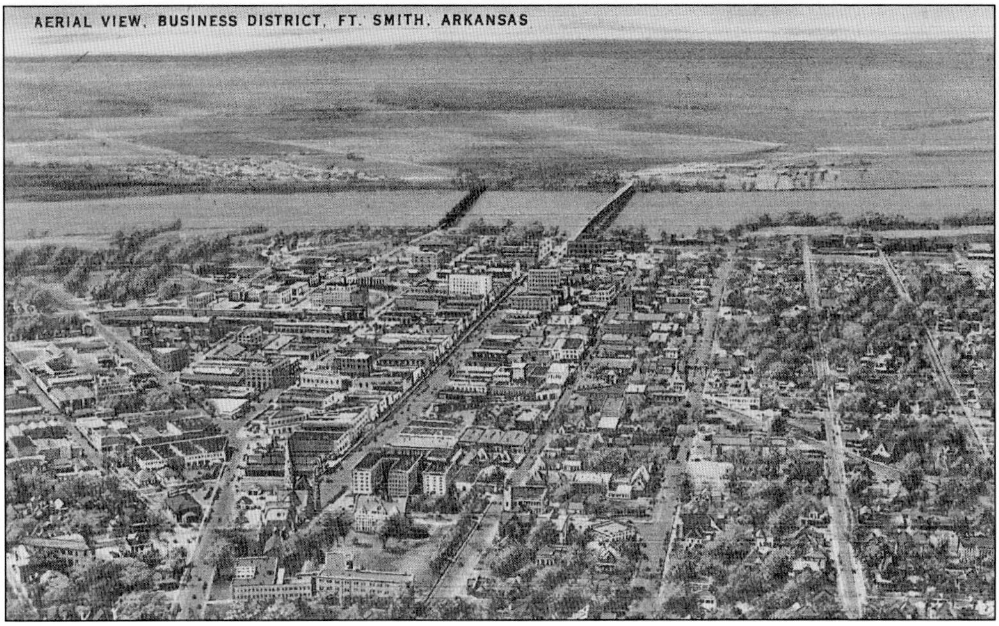

This aerial view of the business district from the 1940s shows the town of Moffett, Oklahoma, across the bridge. Moffett was off-limits to servicemen from Camp Chaffee due to its rowdy reputation. (Fort Smith Public Library Genealogy Department Postcard Collection.)

This postcard advertises one of the areas bringing tourism and business to Arkansas, the Ozark Mountains. Throughout the history of Arkansas, people have traveled to experience the scenic beauty and abundant natural resources in the area. Northwest Arkansas is now one of the fastest-growing areas in the nation. Overall, Arkansas continues to be a national leader in the production of rice, soybeans, corn, cotton, and renewable energy sources. (Fort Smith Public Library Genealogy Department Postcard Collection.)

This 1918 postcard identifies the offices of H.B. Caldwell, the Nathan Clothing Company across the street, and the Hotel Main, as a lady and two men rush to catch a streetcar. (Fort Smith Chamber of Commerce.)

This 1950s view looks westward down Garrison Avenue. The postcard advertises Garrison Avenue, as businesses were booming. Although many changes have come to the area, the Central Business Improvement District has focused on a "Live, Work, Play" agenda to bring residents, businesses, families, and tourism of all kinds back to Garrison Avenue. Businesses offer customer-friendly parking and convenient hours, and the historical location help to bring festivals and various other events year-round. Garrison Avenue is also the home to annual events, including Old Fort Rodeo Days, concerts, farmer's markets, the Fourth of July celebration, history festivals, the St. Patrick's Day festival, and more. (Fort Smith Museum of History.)

"Fort Smith Arkansas: Gateway to the Ozarks" is the title of this souvenir packet sold by D.B. Johnson of Fort Smith in the 1930s. The courthouse behind the monument on the cover was replaced in 1937 with a limestone structure built by the WPA. The soldier's monument reads "Lest We Forget" for his Confederate brethren. (Fort Smith Museum of History.)

The First Presbyterian Church and Sunday school began in 1846. The building pictured here, at North Twelfth Street, opened in 1900. The church also operates Hobson School for preschool and kindergarten students. (Fort Smith Museum of History.)

This view of Garrison from west of Sixth Street offers a comparison with life in 1912. The streetcars have returned to Garrison Avenue and so have the crowds of daily shoppers, businessmen, and travelers. Fort Smith remains a vital hub of activity due to its location on the border with Oklahoma, its proximity to Northwest Arkansas businesses, its natural resources, its transportation opportunities, and its history. (Fort Smith Museum of History.)

The handwritten note on this early-1900s postcard corrects the misidentification of the original quartermaster building from the second Fort Smith as the commissary building. This structure would have been on the south boundary wall of the 1830s structure. Time was not kind to this building, and it fell into disrepair in the 1920s. (Fort Smith Museum of History.)

This 1910-era postcard shows a group of ducks near the old well behind the commissary building. The commissary and quartermaster buildings were often the sites of supply wagons and lines of settlers and natives, who were provided goods from the fort in the 1800s. Around 1910, efforts began to focus on Fort Smith's colorful past to boost civic pride and bring in tourism dollars. Postcards such as this one celebrate the old fort connection. (Fort Smith Museum of History.)

The Iron Mountain/Helen Gould Railway Bridge was built in 1891; the Fort Smith High School was built in 1897, three months before a storm caused massive damage; and St. Anne's Academy was constructed in 1903. The school was renovated and evolved into Darby Junior High School, while the bridge and St. Anne's were demolished in the 1970s. This early postcard promotes the cornerstone values of faith, education, progress, and prosperity, which continue to push Fort Smith forward today. (Stan Kujawa collection.)

Hardscrabble Country Club and Golf Links, seen here in 1933, was built in 1926 on 160 acres. The club hosts the 4-Ball Invitational in addition to many past LPGA and USGA Senior Women's championships and 13 past PGA tournaments. (Fort Smith Museum of History.)

NATURAL DAM NEAR FORT SMITH.

Natural Dam, in the Boston Mountains of the Ozarks, is six miles north of Cedarville and about 20 miles north of Fort Smith. The dam is "200 feet wide [and] spans the entire width of Mountain Fork Creek." There is a picnic area and waterfalls at the dam. (Fort Smith Museum of History.)

This 1908 postcard has the Grand Opera House on the left, with a group of men in conversation on the corner. The building was dedicated in 1887. George Carter, a fireman at the Opera House, was killed during the 1898 tornado. In the 1909 *Julius Cahn-Gus Hill Theatrical Guide*, the Grand is described as charging an admission of 25¢ to $1.50 and offering electric illumination in a "wide proscenium" of 35 feet. There was three feet between curtain line and footlights, and the "distance between side walls [was] 65 feet," with a rigging loft 45 feet from the floor. Additionally, the stage had four trap doors, each measuring eight feet deep. The guide also notes that Fort Smith's population of more than 33,000 had three newspapers: the *Daily Times*, the *News-Record*, and the *Southwest American*. (Fort Smith Museum of History.)

In keeping with the Fort Smith tradition of looking forward to the past, this unique building has been a Methodist Episcopal church and a Knights of Columbus hall and is now the home of Emmy's German Restaurant. Prior to "Emmy's Too" opening here in 2009 under Joe Caldarera, Emmy's was on Eleventh Street from 1962 to 2004, run by Al and Emmy (Werner) Thome. The nearby Jim and Nina Sparks house, built in 1886 on North Fourteenth Street, has been the location of Taliano's Restaurant since 1970, when Tom Caldarera and Jim Cadelli opened the local favorite. (Fort Smith Public Library Genealogy Department Postcard Collection.)

Consistent with our mission to preserve history on a local level, this book was printed in South Carolina on American-made paper and manufactured entirely in the United States. Products carrying the accredited Forest Stewardship Council (FSC) label are printed on 100 percent FSC-certified paper.

MADE IN THE USA